T0328589

Cambridge Elements

Elements of Christianity and Science
edited by
Andrew Davison
University of Cambridge

SCIENCE-ENGAGED THEOLOGY

John Perry
University of St Andrews

Joanna Leidenhag
University of Leeds

CAMBRIDGE
UNIVERSITY PRESS

Shaftesbury Road, Cambridge CB2 8EA, United Kingdom

One Liberty Plaza, 20th Floor, New York, NY 10006, USA

477 Williamstown Road, Port Melbourne, VIC 3207, Australia

314–321, 3rd Floor, Plot 3, Splendor Forum, Jasola District Centre,
New Delhi – 110025, India

103 Penang Road, #05–06/07, Visioncrest Commercial, Singapore 238467

Cambridge University Press is part of Cambridge University Press & Assessment,
a department of the University of Cambridge.

We share the University's mission to contribute to society through the pursuit of
education, learning and research at the highest international levels of excellence.

www.cambridge.org
Information on this title: www.cambridge.org/9781009094054

DOI: 10.1017/9781009091350

First published 2023

A catalogue record for this publication is available from the British Library.

ISBN 978-1-009-09405-4 Paperback
ISSN 2634-3460 (online)
ISSN 2634-3452 (print)

Science-Engaged Theology

Elements of Christianity and Science

DOI: 10.1017/9781009091350
First published online: March 2023

John Perry
University of St Andrews

Joanna Leidenhag
University of Leeds

Author for correspondence: Joanna Leidenhag, j.leidenhag@leeds.ac.uk

Abstract: This Element presents science-engaged theology as a reminder to theologians to use the local tools and products of the sciences as sources for theological reflection. Using critiques of modernity and secularism, the Element questions the idea that Science and Religion were ever transhistorical categories. The Element also encourages theologians to collaborate with colleagues in other disciplines in a highly localized manner that enables theologians to make concrete claims with accountability and show how theological realities are entangled with the empirical world. This title is also available as Open Access on Cambridge Core.

Keywords: science and religion, queen of the sciences, theological sources, natural theology, interdisciplinary

ISBNs: 9781009094054 (PB), 9781009091350 (OC)
ISSNs: 2634-3460 (online), 2634-3452 (print)

Contents

1 Introduction: *Memento Naturam*

Science-engaged theology aims to serve as a reminder to theologians that the local tools and products of the sciences ought to be sources for theological reasoning. Put another way, it leads to better theology if we remember to ask, what methods or tools could help me improve this claim I am making about the empirical world? Often, these will be tools and methods from the sciences.

Theologians make scientific, or science adjacent, claims all the time, particularly when discussing topics like theological anthropology, nature, ecclesiology and ethics.[1] Sometimes these questions will be practical. Can intersex persons be ordained as Roman Catholic priests? Should we give people experiencing a dark night of the soul antidepressants? Is praying for those who persecute you of therapeutic benefit? To answer any of these questions, at the very least, theologians need an accurate and nuanced understanding of the physical and psychological situations at hand. At other times science-engaged theology is not so immediately practical. What are the cognitive processes involved in faith or hope? How do spiritual practices impact character formation? What is God's relationship to more-than-human animals? These are theological questions about empirical realities. The basic principle of science-engaged theology is that whenever theologians make claims about created, empirical realities, they should incorporate the insights of empirical investigation into their analysis.

So, one way to understand the mindset of science-engaged theology is as a way to place scientific research *alongside*, not in competition with, biblical exegesis, the study of history, or philosophical considerations as a ready resource for theological reflection. No self-respecting theologian believes that they can do theology without considering what the Bible or tradition has to say on their chosen topic. We think that theologians should have a similar instinct when drawing on empirical studies.

As Renaissance Christians used art as occasional reminders of mortality, calling them *memento mori*, you could think of science-engaged theology as a *memento naturam*.[2] Needing such occasional mementos isn't at all unprecedented in

---

[1] Barrett 2022.

[2] Of course, this translates as 'remember nature', rather than 'remember scientific tools and findings', but the alternative, *memento scientia*, would be confusing for different reasons. The term science has a complicated backstory. For Aristotle, any system of demonstrably certain knowledge was a science (ἐπιστήμη). Within the medieval university curriculum, a *scientia* was any of the seven liberal arts, sometimes extended to include mathematics and *sacra doctrina*. Based on this, you might expect us to say, 'Theology can be a science too!' That may be true in a sense, but we use science here to mean something narrower. The broader sense is best conveyed by the German *Wissenschaft*, the products of all academic fields including the humanities. We have in mind the narrower sense of empirical investigation, roughly associated with the Scientific Revolution, the discoveries of Galileo and Newton, and the development of various systematic, experimental methods such as Bacon's.

Christian history. When John and Charles Wesley began the Methodist movement, they reminded the church that the experience of the faithful can be a guide and authority for doctrine and practice. When Martin Luther, together with Catholic reformers like Erasmus, advocated for a vernacular Bible, they encouraged remembering Scripture as an authority and source. Reminders are often needed as a corrective, and this is true for science-engaged theology.

Science-engaged theology is a corrective against the tendency for academic specialization to entail ghettoization. Unlike many attempts at interdisciplinarity, we applaud increased expertise and concentration in research, but think this only increases (rather than decreases) the potential for meaningful collaboration. Furthermore, the need for collaboration persists even though specialization in theology often includes highly particular faith commitments that colleagues might not share. This has led some theologians to suggest that confessional theology *belongs* in an intellectual silo, protected from the distorting effects of modernity. On the contrary, science-engaged theology is a reminder that theology is a task best done in diverse community, not only in monastic or church communities but also in multidisciplinary research settings like the university.

As with all human endeavours, there are better and worse ways to do theology, including better and worse ways *to remember that science can be a theological source*. Treating science-engaged theology as a mere slogan would be simplistic. What we mean by 'slogan' here is when a good insight becomes a blunt weapon that flattens a complicated and nuanced picture. Something similar happened to Luther's concept of *sola scriptura*. Luther had a relatively nuanced – at least, nuanced for Luther – understanding of the Bible's place among other sources of theology. This quickly got co-opted into a slogan that would be better named, not *sola*, but *solo scriptura*.[3] For Protestant neo-scholastics and, even nowadays, certain American neo-Calvinists, Luther's reasonable proposal morphed into the unreasonable idea that the Bible can stand alone. Likewise, we do not want science-engaged theology to become a backdoor for naïve scientism within theology. Science does not, and cannot, stand alone. With this cautionary tale in mind, this Element seeks to remind theologians that science ought to count among the sources of Christian theology, while providing clues about how to do this well.

1.1 Three Initial Reactions

Science-engaged theology is far from our own invention.[4] Lots of scholars have recently been calling their work 'science engaged' and, of course, different scholars mean different things by the phrase. Like all concepts, science-engaged

---

[3] Vanhoozer 2005, 154.

[4] Perry and Ritchie 2018 seem to have been the first to use the term in print.

theology emerged from within a community and continues to be shaped by the scholarly interactions of that community. One of the primary purposes of this Element is to allow that community to grow. As such, we thought it helpful to bring readers up to speed by outlining three initial reactions that we have heard over the last few years which have shaped our vision of science-engaged theology. One consequence of this choice, however, is that the remainder of this section jumps directly into some of this Element's thorniest issues, most of which will be returned to with more introductory exposition at later points. Some readers may prefer to jump ahead to Section 1.2.

1.1.1 Well, Obviously

The first reply, the most supportive of our position, could be summarized as, 'well, obviously!'[5] As the rational and personal Creator of the universe, *of course* God speaks through science, and *of course* theologians should listen to all the ways God speaks. Christians have known this for millennia and have studied it systematically since the Middle Ages. In fact, Christian beliefs were a major driver behind scientific pursuits for most of Western history. Why would the church stop now?

We agree! One minor caveat: we should not confuse 'science' used broadly to refer to the way people throughout history and in different cultures have used observational evidence to solve problems, with 'science' used more narrowly, referring to the tradition and social institution with historical roots in sixteenth- and seventeenth-century Europe. Any given Christian – along with well, basically everyone on the planet – understands science differently nowadays than they did in earlier eras; differently, for example, than did medieval Italian priests working in Parisian universities. The difference is one of degree rather than kind, but it is a difference nevertheless – one which is knotted with historical threads that some sections of this Element attempt to unpick. So even those who see science-engaged theology as obvious, us included, could use occasional reminders that God doesn't speak through science without the need for interpretation. As we argue later, what science 'says' is always historically, politically, philosophically and even geographically contingent.

1.1.2 Science Distorts Theology

The second reply is not supportive. It goes something like this: 'science is a corrupt and biased institution. If Christians use the tools of modern science, they will also corrupt theology'. This is a pseudo worry. Most reflective scientists,

---

[5] Grey 2021, 491–2.

such as our university colleagues, *know* that science as an institution is complex and susceptible to corruption and bias. They already take it for granted that scientists disagree with each other, that their findings are always in process and provisional, that the mechanisms of power and prestige play into any equation and that any knowledge we claim to discover is relativized by those facts. But this is true of the humanities (including theology) as well as the sciences.

There is a different version of this objection, which we have heard on more than one occasion, which the final sentence of the previous paragraph may appear to aggravate. This second worry about science potentially distorting theology goes something like this: 'engaging the sciences inevitably puts theology on the back foot and tricks theologians into trying to prove that their claims meet some secular criteria for truth or evidence'. This objection will be dealt with in various places throughout this Element because it is one we are sensitive to and wish to avoid. Science-engaged theology does *not* imply that all theological claims need to be verified, or even corroborated, by the sciences in order to be meaningful or rational. This worry may have been aggravated by the admission in the previous paragraph that theology too is biased and not always reliable. But readers with this concern should note that this comes after agreeing that the sciences are in a similar position. It is, in part, because of universal human fallibility that we think that opening oneself up to multiple sources of correction is an epistemic virtue, and for theologians this includes accountability to empirical inquiry when making empirical claims.

We acknowledge that using the sciences as a source in theology does give science some measure of theological authority. This is not the same as scientism. For a host of reasons explored in later sections, we do not think 'but science says so' should be used as a lazy trump card to win theological debates. So, how much authority *should* theologians give the sciences? In brief, this will depend upon the question one is trying to answer and the theological tradition to which the theologian belongs. It is okay if Mennonites 'remember science' differently than, say, Roman Catholics or Liberal Protestants.

1.1.3 Undermining the Truce

We can introduce the third reply by recounting what has, improbably and somewhat infamously, become a flashpoint for early conversations about science-engaged theology. *Can gluten-free bread be consecrated for the Eucharist?* How could that be contentious? For some critics, the question implies that the sort of problems that science-engaged theology can help with are simply too silly. *What's next, angels dancing on a pin?* Well, if you are a Catholic with coeliac disease, the question is anything but silly; however, we surmise that this objection goes deeper. This is worth considering because we never envisioned this example as the best, most robust kind of science-engaged theology. It is probably better understood as a minimalist example; *at least* everyone can see that organic chemistry (which discovered the protein $C_{24}H_{27}N_5O_9$) can be useful to theology in questions such as these. So when early interlocutors objected even to this, we thought it worth pursuing.

According to some, it seems that our framing of the gluten question imperils the truce between science and religion. For centuries, so the story goes, scholars representing both camps were mistakenly at war. How could you be at war *mistakenly*? Imagine John is the mayor of Cambridge and runs attack ads against Joanna, who he hears also wants to be mayor of Cambridge. Perhaps they each claim that they got the most votes; maybe John even sends the city police after Joanna for the alleged coup. The police find that Joanna *did* get the most votes – in her hometown of Cambridge, England. John, it turns out, was mayor of Cambridge, Massachusetts. The cities should have been at peace all along. So too for the so-called conflict between science and religion. If John claims, 'gravity is a universal force proportional to mass' and Joanna claims, 'God created gravity', our claims are not in conflict. They could have been at peace all along. But *realizing* the war was mistaken after the shooting starts takes lots of peace planning. The truce is fragile; the generals want to keep things going for the military-industrial complex and so on.

If *that* describes the relation of science and religion – a fragile truce after a war where the territories were never in conflict – we can see how asking, 'can gluten-free bread be consecrated?' threatens the hard-won peace. Such a question could (wrongly) be taken to imply that whatever science says about the nature of gluten might somehow dictate Vatican dogma. Since gluten is not in the same conceptual territory as consecration, why confuse matters?

We call this counter argument to our vision for science-engaged theology, *NOMA on steroids*. Non-overlapping Magisteria (NOMA) is the view that theology speaks for values or morality, which aren't empirically discoverable, and science speaks for facts, which are. For many, this division of labour is the basis of the truce; 'Science studies how the heavens go, and theology studies how to go to heaven'. There is some truth behind this cliché. The questions typically asked by empirical scientists are not those typically asked by theologians, and vice versa. Perhaps this is fine some of the time. But the *on steroids* bit gets added when NOMA becomes a hard and fast metaphysical rule. One scientist who espoused this view to us said, 'the Church, being social constructivists *par excellence*, doesn't have to adopt the categories scientists use: a human being is whatever she [the church] says it is, and so is a man or a piece of bread'.

A generation ago, the theologian James Gustafson pejoratively called such thinking, 'Wittgensteinian fideism'.[6] The position holds that the church has its own language game, and all definitions are internal to that game. Whenever Christians say, love or violence or worship or justice, what they mean is 'love', 'violence', 'worship' and 'justice' understood *from within the Christian narrative*. We affirm that theologians must examine the world and everything within it from the perspective of the Christian narrative in all its scandalous particularity. But that narrative does not itself claim to be private, it claims to be universally true and to apply to the physical universe. Far from making theologians rulers of other disciplines, this claim means that theology holds itself partially accountable to the empirical discoveries of others.

Whether we call their position NOMA on steroids or Wittgensteinian fideism, if these critics are right then science-engaged theology is a useless endeavour. Why indeed imperil the truce between science and religion? If, however, the critics are wrong, if there are sound theological reasons against such views – as we argue – then the discipline of theology could very much use a *memento naturam*; a reminder that science is one of the ways that Christians have learned to listen to God.

1.2 Science-Engaged Theology Done Well

In Section 1, we wrote that we don't want our reminder to be simplistic, such as could happen if it became a mere slogan. Christians have more or less always seen the science of the day as a source for theology, but since the dawn of modernity, and especially since 1800 or so, a series of debates have muddied these waters. It would be naïve of us to simply endorse using science as a source for theology without consideration of these muddy waters, and likewise naïve to overlook the work that already has been done to clear the water – which has made science-engaged theology possible. We want to fill in all this background before giving our positive account of what science-engaged theology is in Section 5. It is helpful to phrase these prior debates as three questions, each of which we will address in a section of this Element.

- How can theologians use science as a source given the apparent fragile truce/ war between science and religion? We will answer this question in Section 2 by discussing how science-engaged theology relates to the pre-existing field of science and religion.
- How can theologians employ scientific tools given theology's marginal place in the modern university? In Section 3, we make an intervention into these

---

[6] Gustafson 2013, but the term is originally from Nielsen 1967.

ongoing debates about the identity and position of theology in relation to other disciplines.

• What is it that theology is meant to engage with? We will explore the question of scientific unity and disunity in Section 4 with the help of twentieth-century philosophy of science.

Having cleared these muddy waters our constructive proposal is built in response to a further three questions. Why science? What is a source? How should this source be used, exactly? In Section 5, we speak more positively of what it means to remember that the sciences are among the sources of theology.

Our overall argument might be summarized in the following way. It turns out that the much-hyped war/truce between 'science' and 'religion' is not what it appears, because these disciplines are not two distinct natural kinds or transhistorical categories, but socially contingent groupings of diverse and intertwined knowledge-seeking enterprises. On the one hand, some have used science as a proxy for rationality or emancipation and religion as a proxy for superstition and oppression. On the other hand, others have sought to declare theology queen of the sciences. Only after dissolving these petty power plays can we see that science-engaged theology is a sign of theologians' quiet confidence in their position in the university. Developments in twentieth-century philosophy of science strengthen this claim further by speaking of the plurality of the sciences. The sciences only *appear* unified through the disjunctive continuity established by trading zones and pidgin languages. These are the spaces and skills that science-engaged theologians should seek to join and practise.

Science-engaged theology is a disposition for theologians to modestly use the best available tools when making empirical claims, alongside (and not in competition with) all the other sources and tools that a theologian uses to know God and all things in relation to God. We provide short examples of science-engaged theology by incorporating weblinks to the work of others throughout our text; offline readers will find the links collected in the appendix.[7] Using science as a source is one thing, doing so well is far more difficult. To that end, we conclude this Element with rules of thumb to point out where the pitfalls lie and how to best avoid them.

2 Beyond the Territories of Science and Religion

We've all heard that science and religion have been at war. And in dialogue. And have nothing to do with each other. So, which is it? Scholars have been asking this question for a while now; we ought to have some idea. Almost a century ago, here's how Alfred North Whitehead began an article in *The Atlantic*:

---

[7] Sometimes these examples exemplify something we are discussing in the main body of the text, at other points the link is more tenuous. We advise readers not to overthink their placement.

> The difficulty in approaching the question of the relation between Religion and Science is that its elucidation requires that we have in our minds some clear idea of what we mean by either of the terms, 'religion' and 'science'. Also I wish to speak in the most general way possible, and to keep in the background any comparison of particular creeds, scientific or religious. We have to understand the type of connection which exists between the two spheres, and then to draw some definite conclusions respecting the existing situation which at present confronts the world.[8]

Here, Whitehead typifies the way that many have approached the question: look for some lowest common denominator that lies at the core of 'religion' and 'science' to make sense of the relation between these monoliths of human civilization. Leave the scientific and religious specifics out of it because what we are looking for is an essential core. Keep it generic.

We will not judge whether this plan ever made sense, but this Element advocates a different approach. Instead of keeping 'particular creeds, scientific or religious' in the background as Whitehead wanted, science-engaged theology keeps them front and centre. Rather than a school or method, science-engaged theology is a mindset which any theologian of any camp or tradition could (and we think should) adopt. Theologians do not need to set aside their particular faith and denominational concerns and commitments. The mindset of science-engaged theology can be expressed as when a theologian asks a simple question: what methods or tools could help me improve this claim I am making about the world?

We agree with Whitehead, however, that you can't study everything all at once, so our approach leaves some things out too. What we strive to 'keep in the background' is precisely the search for a core. Why? First, because we doubt there is any essential core to be found in categories as broad as religion and science. Second, because the quest for the essence of 'science' or of 'religion' has been politicized throughout modernity. We cannot study what's essential to this or that concept without also asking who benefits from using that label. Finally, looking for cores to science and religion, as Whitehead does, prioritizes certain archetypal cases that make a generic relation most obvious, either with now-clichéd anecdotes of conflict ('Christians believed the earth was flat until Columbus') or independent harmony ('science studies how the heavens go, religion how to go to heaven'). While they may have started as historical episodes, such archetypal cases are often mythologized by science and religion discourse, such that they bare little relevance or similarity to the daily mess of theological or scientific enquiry.

It has been a century since Whitehead posed his question – what is the relation between science and religion? – and it's now common for scholars to admit that

---

[8] Whitehead 1925.

it cannot be categorized as one simple story or metanarrative. Are they in conflict or can they help each other out, or do science and religion simply ask different questions? Yes. And yes and yes. History is always messier than the easy tropes we find so useful. But can we say more than, 'it's ... complicated'? We think so. In fact, the goal of this section is to tell the stories behind the story of why it's so complex, why we can say more and begin to explain why science-engaged theology isn't, and shouldn't be, about how 'science' and 'religion' relate.

The history of science and religion is best told not as a story about Galileo, Newton and Darwin, but as a story about the stories we have told and continue to tell of these two disciplines: in other words, a historiography. As Peter Harrison argues, science and religion are not transhistorical categories that we can track throughout different epochs, but imagined concepts that, as a result of certain theories of secularism, have come to be defined in opposition. Even though the myth of conflict has been abandoned by all serious historians, as long as we are asking questions about how something called 'science' relates to something called 'religion', we are setting the stage for misunderstandings, misconceptions and myths.

In this section, we answer the question posed in the introduction: how can theologians use science as a source given the apparent fragile war/truce between science and religion? Our answer is organized under three headings. First, Double Mythbusting (Section 2.1) challenges the appearance of a fragile war/truce. We argue that the 'war' and 'truce' purport to be myths of *history* but are, in fact, built on myths of *historiography*. Second, Countless Typologies (Section 2.2) argues that the enthusiasm in the field of science and religion for building typologies has been a misguided attempt to grapple with the consequences of an increasingly complex picture. Third (Section 2.3), we use the arguments of three Gifford lecture series, by prominent historians and geographers of science, to explain how science-engaged theology hopes to move beyond the acknowledgement of complexity onto something more constructive.

2.1 Double Mythbusting: The Myths (of the Myths) of Conflict and NOMA

We are not opposed to myths. As teachers, how could we be? Myths allow stories to convey lessons. Even apocryphal stories can be useful; the problem with myths is not necessarily their grounding in history. Whether or not Laplace ever told Napoleon, 'I have no need of that hypothesis', it can be a useful teaching tool to express the concern that the Newtonian universe can lead to Deism. Nor is it a problem that myths simplify complex stories. Good teachers simplify and narrate; it's how teaching works. On the other hand, some myths include implicit lessons that the teacher does not intend, and the result is that the student is misled. The more often the teacher tells the myth, the more likely it is that they too are being misled by their own pedagogy.

2.1.1 The Myth of Conflict

In this section, we look at how the myths of science and religion, of which the conflict thesis is only the most well-known, are created by making smaller stories paradigmatic for a larger narrative. Put simply, the myth of conflict holds that science and religion are wholly incompatible such that individuals and societies must choose a side. This dichotomy is propped up by the oversimplification, and sometimes outright misrepresentation, of individual historical episodes or debates: the discovery that the Earth is not flat, Galileo's imprisonment for teaching heliocentrism, the notion that religions assumed poor mental health was demonic possession until the advent of modern psychiatry, the idea that you can't believe in God and evolution at the same time. Each of these individual debates are massaged to fit into a predetermined metanarrative of inevitable conflict between two eternal monoliths, 'Science' and 'Religion'.

For example, in his influential *History of the Conflict between Religion and Science* (1875), John William Draper tells the story of how 'the theological doctrine of the flatness of the earth was irretrievably overthrown' by the voyages of Columbus and Magellan. Here we have a clear Whiggish history of inevitable scientific progress, and it seems that such progress must be made at the expense of religion. Draper writes, the 'irreligious tendency [of Columbus' planned voyage] was pointed out by the Spanish ecclesiastics and condemned by the Council of Salamanca' using Scripture and the Church Fathers.[9] Draper's account is mostly nonsense, of course. The shape of the Earth had been well established, including among Christians, since at least the 600s – so nearly a millennium before Columbus – and among some Greeks, a millennium before that. But the story goes that Draper's book, together with White's *A History of the Warfare of Science with Theology in Christendom* (1896), founded what historians came to call the conflict thesis or conflict model.

In due course, historians realized that the conflict thesis was more like a conflict myth. Draper and White invented whole episodes and took quotes out of context, which is ably summarized in Ronald Numbers' *Galileo Goes to Jail* and elsewhere.[10] Few scholars since the 1980s consider either Draper or White to be reliable sources. By showing that the promoters of the conflict model 'read the past through battle-scarred glasses', Numbers and the other

---

[9] Draper 1875, 160–1.

[10] Numbers 2009. And elsewhere, including Lindberg and Numbers 1986, 140–9.

historians who realized this were performing one level of mythbusting.[11] By this we mean, the historical events and narratives (Galileo and Columbus) don't demonstrate what the mythmakers (Draper and White) claim.

However, it turns out that we need a kind of double mythbusting here, because other thinkers – popularizers – turned the *mythmakers* into myths of their own. Not only is the conflict model unsupported by historical evidence, but *Draper and White never advocated the conflict model themselves*, if by conflict we mean that science and religion are inevitably at war. Instead, both Draper and White claimed only that *some* theologians – some well-meaning but confused, others seeking political power – *created* conflict where there should have been none. For Draper, the conflict 'commenced when Christianity began to attain political power', which he equated with Roman Catholicism; he had little problem with Protestant churches, provided they adhered to the principles of the Reformation (as he understood those principles).[12] White's own conflict model also developed over the years. Science faced narrower and narrower rivals: 'from "religion" in 1869, to "ecclesiasticism" in 1876 . . . and finally to "dogmatic theology"'.[13] With what he deemed the true heart of the Christian faith, White saw no conflict. What we mean by 'double mythbusting' here is that the conflict thesis lacks historical support *and* this myth's putative founders held middle-of-the-road, turn-of-the-century east coast, theological views in the tradition of Walter Rauschenbusch, Charles Augustus Briggs and Henry Ward Beecher. By this measure, Draper's and White's argument was never about interdisciplinary conflict, per se. It was about pushing theology in a liberal direction, in keeping with their fellow New Yorkers and the wider tradition of liberal Protestantism in Europe.

2.1.2 The Myth of NOMA

The conflict model is not the only source of problematic myths. Sometimes even useful myths can get co-opted by popularizers who apply them sloppily. Stephen Jay Gould was the highest-profile scientist to first follow the historians and argue that the conflict model doesn't line up with history.[14] In his essay, 'The Late Birth of a Flat Earth', he wrote of 'the construction, by Draper and White, of the mythical model of warfare between science and religion – a model that must be debunked for the NOMA principle to prevail'.[15]

The NOMA principle, short for 'Non-overlapping Magisteria', originated in Gould's thoughtful comparison on teachings of Darwinian evolution by Pius XXI and John Paul II. This essay argued, as John Henry Newman had a century

---

[11] Lindberg and Numbers 1986, 141.   [12] Draper 1875, v–xvi.
[13] Lindberg and Numbers 1986, 140.   [14] Gould 2002, 103–106.   [15] Gould 1995, 92–3.

earlier, that science and religion 'on the whole, are incommunicable, incapable of collision'.[16] Gould's work ironically turned into a myth too. Gould gives an emphatic 'No' to a clear borderline, but others – popularizers again – have turned Gould's NOMA into a myth. Sometimes this is referred to in typologies as 'independence'. For example, *if* the full extent of the principle is captured by Gould's assertion that 'the net of science covers the empirical universe ... The net of religion extends over questions of moral meaning and value', NOMA is merely a version of the so-called fact-value division, and all science and religion conflicts are instances of the naturalistic fallacy. This misreading of Gould is found in figures as different as (notoriously) Dawkins' *God Delusion* and Alister McGrath's *Dawkins Delusion*.[17]

'A magisterium', Gould explains, 'is a domain where one form of teaching holds the appropriate tools for meaningful discourse and resolution'.[18] Maybe Gould should have used another word rather than magisterium, such as practice, sub-discourse or tradition. Gould's point is not about division, isolation or even independence. Gould's real point is about finding the best *match* between, on the one hand, the tools and the tradition of discourse we use to reason together about such tools, and, on the other hand, the questions we ask with these tools and the findings we derive from them. That Gould didn't intend anything like Dawkins' simplistic, fact-value misreading could not be clearer.

> This resolution might remain all neat and clean if the nonoverlapping magisteria (NOMA) of science and religion were separated by an extensive no man's land. But, in fact, the two magisteria bump right up against each other, interdigitating in wondrously complex ways along their joint border. Many of our deepest questions call upon aspects of both for different parts of a full answer – and the sorting of legitimate domains can become quite complex and difficult.[19]

An example of how science and theology can interdigitate can be seen in Joshua Cockayne's and Gideon Salter's work.[20] Here memory seems to be an entangled concept, where biblical exegesis, philosophy and psychology are all needed to answer the question: What does it mean to 'remember' biblical events during corporate acts of worship?

Gould still speaks of a (shared and unclear) border between exactly two (vaguely) identifiable camps, but we read him as struggling to *overcome* the idea

---

[16] Newman 1979, 431. Although, given Newman's ideal of a Catholic university as a multidisciplinary conversation and with the sciences ordered towards true piety, 'independence' hardly applies to Newman either.

[17] McGrath 2007, 18. McGrath corrected his mistake in later publications.   [18] Gould 1995, 5.

[19] Gould 2011, 274. Gould admittedly creates some confusion for himself.

[20] Cockayne and Salter 2021.

that we can identify where science begins and religion ends. If this is an attempt to overcome such a binary conceptualization, then it is ironic that Gould has come to represent the idea that science and religion are independent from one another. Instead, where Gould speaks of science and theology as 'interdigitating', we have come to speak of, and seek out, 'entangled concepts'. Entangled concepts are concepts that cannot be understood as either scientific or theological in meaning and origin, but only as both.

Let us summarize this double mythbusting section. Many people have been taught to think of science and religion as relating in one of two ways, either in conflict or independently of each other: the Conflict model and the NOMA model. Furthermore, each has been associated with a historical figure or tradition, which serves to lend it legitimacy: Draper and White, and Gould. The Conflict and NOMA models never made much historical sense (myth level 1) and were never held by Draper and White or Gould anyway (myth level 2). Gould's more sophisticated (non-slogan) version of NOMA is surprisingly perceptive. Yet the perceptive version's strength is its complexity, which in tricky cases, may struggle to say much beyond, 'The relationship is ... complicated'.

2.2 Countless Typologies

The relationship between science and religion can be construed in many different ways, depending on the stories that you take as paradigmatic, or the historical event that you invest with mythological significance. Clearly there are more options on the table than the two models cited in the last section.

One of the ways that this field has tried to handle such an unruly and contentious history is to create typologies that simplify and organize the various stories into stable categories. The most famous typology, which in a sense founded 'science and religion' as its own academic discipline, is Ian Barbour's fourfold typology: conflict, independence, dialogue and integration.[21] Barbour's typology has been undeniably useful as a tool for challenging the monolith of the myth of conflict and reaching wider audiences because of its simplicity.[22] The possibility of conflict was maintained, but it was no longer the dominant theme. It is, therefore, unsurprising that since Barbour, anyone who is anyone in science and religion has tried their hand at the typology game.

---

[21] Barbour 1966; 1974; Barbour's 'Ways of Relating Science and Religion' was first published in 1988, expanded slightly in *Religion in an Age of Science* (1990) and *Religion in an Age of Science as Religion and Science* (1997), and used to restructured his 1990 Gifford lectures into a 2000 popular monograph, *When Science Meets Religion: Enemies, Strangers, or Partners?*

[22] See the criticism Barbour's typology has received from historians. Cantor and Kenny 2001, 765–81.

Throughout the 1980s and 1990s scholars made minor adjustments to the basic fourfold typology, seeking to account for historical complexity simply by adding more types or sub-types. In the 1980s Arthur Peacocke published an eightfold typology, which Robert Russell reformatted into a 'four-dimensional model which allows for a continuum between opposite positions'.[23] Nancey Murphy appropriated H. Richard Niebuhr's classic culture and theology typology for science and theology, hoping that theology could transform science.[24] In 1995, John Haught developed a fourfold (and alliterative!) typology: conflict, contrast, contact and confirmation, which closely paralleled Barbour.[25] Willem Drees offered a ninefold typology in 1996 that sought to show new ideas interact with different areas where science and religion overlap.[26] In 1997, Philip Clayton constructed a sevenfold typology around the power relations between science and theology.[27] Ted Peters' 1998 eightfold typology distinguished between scientific materialists and scientific imperialists, as well as between Roman Catholic authoritarianism and Protestant fundamentalism.[28] In 2004, John Polkinghorne tried to keep it simple by returning to a fourfold typology (deistic, theistic, revisionary and developmental). Polkinghorne saw all his categories as sub-categories within Barbour's previous 'dialogue' type, which differed on theological method and epistemology.

By the turn of the century, constructing a new typology was becoming an increasingly complicated task. In 2010, Mikael Stenmark published a (very sophisticated) typology of all these typologies! Alvin Plantinga's 2011 *Where the Conflict Really Lies* is slightly different, designed to make the argument that it is naturalism, and not natural science, that is incompatible with Christian theology. Plantinga's contribution highlights that, despite appearances, typologies are not neutral. Like all maps, typologies prioritize some features, erase others and convey normative arguments. The most recent book-length typology is Neil Messer's *Science in Theology*.[29] The quest for the perfect typology has dominated the field of science and religion for several decades.

Typologies are not in themselves bad, but with such a proliferation, we should step back and evaluate their effect. There are three particularly interesting results from all this. The first is that when typologists organize various paradigmatic stories into separate categories, they perpetuate old myths and even create myths of their own. Contrary to his status as the poster-boy for the independence type, Gould's famous essay, 'Non-overlapping Magisteria' is about the entanglements at the borders, *not* an apology for clear territories.[30] Draper writes of an 'antagonism' between 'two contending powers' but these powers

---

[23] Peacocke 1981, xiii–xv; Russell 1985; Peacocke responded to Russell: Peacocke 1993, 20–1.
[24] Murphy 1985, 16–23.   [25] Haught 1995, ch. 1.   [26] Drees 1996, 39–53.
[27] Clayton 1998.   [28] Peters 1998, 13–22.   [29] Messer 2020.   [30] Gould 1997.

are *not* science and religion, but the political powers that had co-opted Christianity. Typologies are a way to standardize the stories that we tell about the stories *and* cast the storytellers into simple heroes and villains.

The second result of the age of typologies is a growing distinction between historical description and normative argument. Typologies create a buffet of choices for how the reader *wants* the fields to relate. It challenges the monolithic myth of conflict not by questioning the historicity of the paradigmatic stories of conflict in the past, but by offering alternative possibilities. The rhetorical move here is to say, '*So what* if the Church put Galileo on trial? That was then; now we are opened-minded and interdisciplinary. We have the choice to carve out a different future where science and religion unite – provided religion has learnt its lesson'. This co-opts the myth of progress in order to regain some modest place for religion in a scientific world. It is for this reason that typologies have been useful to the apologetic impulse within the science-and-religion field and also why they continuously place theology on the back foot. It must be emphasized that while typologies aim to create more choices, they can simultaneously limit the scope of possibility by giving pre-set options.

The third result, as exemplified in Stenmark's work, is an increasing awareness that it is not only the relationship between science and religion that is up for debate, but that 'science' and 'religion' themselves are contested categories. If this logic is followed, it starts to erode the whole typology game.[31] Despite all the attempts to improve on Barbour, the reliance on typologies has entrenched another myth; the myth of science and religion as natural kinds or transhistorical categories.

> *One of the clearest arguments against fitting theology and empirical sciences neatly into just one box in some typology is Tasia Scrutton's article.[32] Could a period of mental distress be both a Dark Night of the Soul and mental illness at the same time?*

Science-engaged theology should not be conceived as just another category within some wider typological framework. If the claim of science-engaged theology was *only* that theologians should use science as a source for theological research, then this might be a sub-category of the dialogue or integration types. But we have in mind a science-engaged theology that goes a step further by embracing the inherent instability of 'science' and 'religion' as continually contested and entangled concepts. As such, it is important to recognize that science-engaged theology necessitates a theology of science. That is, an interrogation of the metaphysical foundations for what we happen to call 'science' here and now on a global level.

---

[31] On the question of natural kinds, see Rorty 1988, 49–74.   [32] Scrutton 2021.

We hope that this will further encourage a theology-engaged science, where scientists engage in theological-philosophical reflection on the concepts and methods they use on a local level.

2.3 It's Complicated! An Englishman, an Irishman and an Australian

Bernard Lightman aptly summarizes what happened next among historians of science and religion: 'instead of uncritically accepting it as an accurate description of what had occurred in the past, scholars began to treat the conflict thesis itself as a product of history, constructed by historical actors, and therefore requiring analysis'.[33] The consequences of this move – which essentially proposed seeing the conflict model, and by extension other types, as *products* of historiographical manufacture – served to bolster a new thesis among these historians. This new thesis could be called, *It's . . . complicated.*

And those historians are right; it is complicated! However, in the words of Ronald Numbers, 'complexifying history seems to have little to recommend it besides its truth . . . the turn to complexity has left most people yawning'.[34] Sometimes boring truth is exactly what's needed. Still, can we say more than 'It's complicated' without reverting back to, 'Science and religion interact in exactly x number of ways'? Yes we can. Numbers pursued the mythbusting strategy (see his trademark book, *Galileo Goes to Jail*), but he also searched for what he called 'mid-scale patterns'.[35] Mid-scale patterns fall short of proposing a timeless metanarrative like Conflict or Harmony, but still assert discernible themes or trends within the contingencies of history.[36]

Our approach may at first glance look much the same as Numbers' twofold strategy (mythbusting and mid-scale narratives), but we think we can go yet another step further. We can best introduce our approach by reference to three Gifford lecturers who all have contributed to what has been called, 'the gospel of complexity'.[37] From three recent Gifford lecturers – an Englishman, an Irishman and an Australian – we have found a version of complexity that we can sign up to defend *and* that shows why a different approach to the whole idea of science and religion is needed. John Hedley Brooke, David Livingstone and Peter Harrison each add a layer to the story and, taken together, they offer a way to progress beyond the study of 'science' and 'religion', thus conceived.

---

[33] Lightman 2019, 4.   [34] Numbers 2010, 263–4.   [35] Numbers 2010, 263–82.

[36] For a careful analysis and critique of Numbers mid-scale patterns, see Stenhouse 2019, ch. 4. For secularization as a mid-scale pattern, see Harrison 2015.

[37] Numbers 2010, 269: 'without abandoning the gospel of complexity and retreating to uncomplicated master-narratives we can . . . search for mid-scale patterns, whether epistemic or social, demographic or geographical, theological or scientific'.

2.3.1 John Hedley Brooke and Geoffrey Cantor, Reconstructing Nature

Perhaps the most notorious story upon which the myth of conflict has been built is when the Vatican forced – or was it excommunicated or tortured or imprisoned? – Galileo to renounce the Copernican system because it contradicted the Bible. In his first Gifford lecture, John Hedley Brooke plays a game of 'who said it?' He asked readers to guess which of the following quotes was Galileo and which was Cardinal Bellarmine who presided over the famous trial of 1616. The first quote, seemingly the more liberal, simply states: 'if there were a true demonstration ... [that] the earth circles the sun, then one would have to ... say rather that we do not understand [the Scriptures]'. In short, trust any 'true demonstration' and be willing to reinterpret Scripture. The second quote reads: 'if they [propositions about nature] contain anything contrary to the Holy Writ, then they must be considered indubitably false and must be demonstrated such by every possible means'.[38] Of course, Brooke's punchline is that the first quote, prescribing biblical reinterpretation in light of true demonstrations, was Cardinal Bellarmine and the second, more reactionary, quotation was Galileo. The point is not only to show how simplistic many of the stories about this episode are but also to illustrate the silliness of lifting quotes out of their historical, biographical, geographical and political contexts.

This anecdote demonstrates Brooke's version of complexity: science and religion studies must use the full complement of the historian's toolkit. Brooke construes the historian's task over and against the tendency to rely on just-so stories to create master-narratives or typologies. As he puts it: 'there are many stories to be told ... they cannot correctly be reduced to over-arching schemata, such as those based on conflict or harmony'.[39] Historians have standard methods of gaining access to these stories, such as contextual history, which we saw Brooke demonstrate . If we think that 'science' versus 'religion' explains Galileo versus Bellarmine, we are doomed to misunderstanding. Instead, *context* matters: what was the power structure at the Vatican in this day? Was Bellarmine simply a hothead; was Galileo naïve? In addition to contextual history, Brooke lists other approaches that are especially important to historical study in this field: functional, linguistic, biographical, social, contextual and practical.

The above should explain why our approach could, at first glance, look like Numbers' strategy. Viewed from a certain point, the tools of the historian Brooke lists are the basis of mid-scale patterns, so from Numbers' perspective this verifies his approach. Add more and more tools generating more and more patterns and eventually you will have no more to say than simply, 'How do science and religion relate? You know ... it's complicated'. However, viewed

---

[38] Brooke and Cantor 1998, 24.   [39] Brooke and Cantor 1998, 8.

from *our* perspective, Brooke's approach drives more nails in the coffin of even being able to ask Whitehead's question. Whereas Whitehead implies that you can't understand how science and religion relate until you settle on the core of each, we join Brooke in saying, the full range of the historians' tools make it 'extremely difficult, if not impossible, for the historian to sympathise with projects designed to uncover the essence of "science," the essence of "religion" and therefore of some timeless, inherent "relationship" between them'.[40]

2.3.2 *David Livingstone,* Putting Science in its Place

Whereas Brooke uses the tools of a historian, our second lecturer, David Livingstone creates a 'geography of science-and-religion'.[41] In his 2014 Gifford lectures *Dealing with Darwin*, Livingstone conducts an interesting experiment. Like any good experiment, he stabilizes many of the variables to test one hypothesis: *place* plays an irreducibly important role in the encounter between science and religion. To test this hypothesis, Livingstone stabilizes (1) the historical period, focusing on the turn of the last century, (2) the scientific theory under consideration, by only investigating the reaction to Darwin's theory of natural selection and (3) the theological tradition, by examining Scottish Calvinists spread across the globe. What were the results of this experiment?

In New Zealand, Presbyterians *supported* Darwin's theory of natural selection because they found in it 'a heartlessly robust selectionism that supported cutthroat ethics of race and class struggle'.[42] They reasoned – even sometimes in these words[43] – if British colonialism causes the Māori to die out, it's not *our* fault; it's God's plan at work. Only the fittest survive. Whereas in the United States, the Presbyterians of Charleston, South Carolina *opposed* Darwin because the evolutionary monogenism of natural selection didn't fit well with segregationist politics.[44] We find different results again in Edinburgh, Belfast, Toronto and Princeton.

It might be tempting to assume that place and local sociopolitical dynamics impact the 'religion' side of the equation far more than the 'science' side. After all, natural selection is as true in Auckland as it is in Charleston, and the difference in interpretation is an issue of values and ethics only, right? In his earlier *Putting Science in its Place*, Livingstone dissolves such a view by exploring how the sites of production (the laboratory, the zoo, the hospital and the field) determine what kind of scientific knowledge is produced. Indeed, the reason science seems so universal is because deliberate effort is made to replicate or homogenize the spaces of investigation. At a larger level of scale, regions of the world can be meaningfully

---

[40] Brooke and Cantor 1998, 10.   [41] Livingstone 2014, 25.   [42] Livingstone 2014, 18.
[43] Giles 1863, 549.   [44] Livingstone 2014, 122.

said to have different sciences.[45] Different forms of patronage, traditions of education, mechanisms for communicating ideas and social structures all influence what counts as a scientific activity, what questions can be asked, what methods are deemed appropriate, how a discovery is justified, how trustworthy the endeavour is taken to be. And as we've seen in the story of how Darwinism spread across the world, 'migration is not replication'; as scientific ideas, apparatus, texts and institutions spread across the world, they are changed.[46]

To be clear, the replication of experiments and findings in different places is a remarkable achievement of science and adds to its trustworthiness as a knowledge-seeking practice. However, as Livingstone reminds us, 'internationalism in science ... must be considered a social achievement, not the inevitable consequence of some inherent scientific essence'.[47] As with Brooke's proposal, we interpret the results of Livingstone's geographical experiment as demonstrating – yet again – that the search for a definitive relation between science and religion is a dead end. Livingstone sensibly concludes, science (thus stated) and religion (thus stated) don't relate in a single way, or even a host of ways. They are not trans*geographical* categories.

2.3.3 *Peter Harrison,* Territories of Science and Religion

Our third Gifford lecturer, Peter Harrison, asks us to imagine hearing of a hitherto unknown conflict between medieval Israel and medieval Egypt. Such a conflict would be impossible because neither Israel nor Egypt existed at this time. While the territories – rivers, mountains and coastlines – existed, the borders between them and the self-conscious identities of nation states did not. The same, he suggests, can be said of science and religion. Before the modern period, and perhaps even as late as the mid-nineteenth century, it was impossible for there to have been a conflict, or dialogue, or even independence between science and religion. Harrison explains this by showing how in the medieval period the terms *scientia* and *religio* were primarily understood as internal virtues or personal qualities. It was only after these terms came to refer to external practices or bodies of knowledge that it was even possible to ask: what's the relationship between science and religion?

---

[45] Livingstone argues that we can, and maybe should, speak not of 'science' but 'speak of Chinese science under the Sung emperors, Arabic science under the patronage of Abassid caliph al-Mansur, American science in the age of Jackson, or French science in the late Enlightenment. Equally, we can plausibly refer to "Edinburgh science" in Enlightenment Scotland, "London science" in the early Victorian period, or "Charleston science" in antebellum America'. Livingstone 2003, 89.
[46] Livingstone 2003, 11.   [47] Livingstone 2003, 89.

The story of 'science and religion' *is* indeed complex. It had many conflicts and instances of harmony and cannot be understood via any one overarching model, but neither is it enough to simply point to the diversity. If the former invites misunderstanding, the latter risks giving up on any kind of understanding at all. Lightman writes: 'the primary task of the historian is not the searching out of complexity per se, but the attempt to render complexity intelligible as far as that is possible. This brings me to a consideration of the one pattern that both Numbers and Brooke identified as a candidate for bringing some level of coherence to our historical understandings – secularization'.[48]

For any theologian working today, any attention to the backstories of terms like science and religion will immediately sound alarm bells and raise red flags. Why? Because theologians have learned from a host of scholars – MacIntyre, Taylor, Hauerwas and Tanner to name a few – that the act of naming something 'scientific' or 'religious' is very often part of an ideological power play. This view was perhaps most memorably stated by William Cavanaugh; what Cavanaugh says about *religio* and *status* in the so-called wars of religion closely mirrors what Harrison says about *religio* and *scientia* in the so-called war of science with theology.[49] Secularization might look like just another mid-level pattern, but it is more than this. It is a way of deconstructing the very terms under investigation.

We began this section by asking, *Sure, the relation of science and religion is complex, but where do we go now?* Harrison points us in the direction of 'the construction of a new kind of metanarrative – "meta" in the sense that it does not take the categories for granted, but rather stands above them and seeks to offer a historical account of *how we came to think in those terms in the first place*'.[50] How, indeed? It is not only misleadingly simplistic to tell the story of Galileo or Columbus as a story of conflict between 'science and religion', thereby ignoring other forces at play, but it is even more deeply anachronistic than that. The mismatch between modern categories and historical events can create a façade of historical complexity, and hide the simpler, truer story from view.[51]

Brooke's tactic was to erode the smaller stories which have been used to create the grand myths of science and religion, thereby disavowing any claims of a master narrative. By contrast, Harrison's version of historical complexity includes the mandate for scholars to propose genealogical metanarratives that make the complexities of the past intelligible. What Harrison does then is to tell the story of science and religion, where these are changing rather than static concepts, by subsuming this story within larger accounts of secularization and the loss of Aristotelian-Thomistic teleology.

---

[48] Harrison 2019, 226.   [49] Cavanaugh 1995, 397–420; 2009.
[50] Harrison 2019, 234, emphasis added.   [51] Harrison 2019.

2.4 Conclusion

This section sought to answer the question: how can theologians engage science given the apparently fragile war or truce, between science and religion? The first part of our answer explored the myths behind the idea of either a war or a truce. The second part of our answer argued that no matter how carefully you negotiate, no matter how subtle your typology, this approach is riddled with myths that need to be deconstructed. The third part of our answer used the work of three historians to show one way that such a deconstruction might proceed. Simply put, the categories of science and religion, as they are understood in much contemporary discourse, are deeply misleading. Science-engaged theology is not simply another way of describing Ian Barbour's category of dialogue since dialogue supposes discrete conversation partners.

3 Neither Serf Nor Queen: Theology's New Boldness in the University

The question, 'How does science relate to religion?' led scholars down blind alleys and into dead ends. We need to deconstruct the ways that modernity used the concepts, 'science' and 'religion' as badges or ciphers to separate rationality from irrationality. The reason the Conflict model still haunts us is that this myth was never about actual instances of disagreement, but about rival theories of knowledge and authority. The Conflict model was a proxy for an older debate, one that is quintessentially a part of the political, cultural and philosophical shifts that came to be known as modernity.

Compare two episodes. As Numbers shows, the Galileo-Bellarmine dispute is partly due to the personalities involved and the intra-Vatican politics of the day. This is historically interesting, perhaps, but not necessarily indicative of a larger trend. However, when Thomas Jefferson writes, the 'monkish ignorance' of religion is now squashed by 'the light of science' *that* is something different – or so we shall argue. So, again, the deconstruction of modern terms like 'science' is necessary because in this conversation the terms were *invented* as tools of an ideology called secularism. The putative relation of inevitable Conflict then became the evidence that adherents of secularism like Jefferson offered. In Section 3.1, we see that the intellectual descendants of Jefferson, who police the border between science and superstition, are still with us. The most striking example is offered by Russell McCutcheon, a scholar of the scientific study of religion. McCutcheon speaks for many critics of theology when he writes: 'simply put, the future of the human sciences are at stake' if theologians – insiders, as he puts it – count as legitimate academics.[52]

For a time, theologians played into that demand. They limited themselves to foundationalist protectionism or retreated into a realm of private spirituality. In effect, they either said, 'theology can play by the rules of Jefferson's science too!' or 'theology is a private matter'. One young Swiss theologian refused to play this game. As explored in Section 3.2, various strands of post-Barthian theology have sought to recover theology's voice in the modern university by emphasizing that all knowledge is traditioned and must be evaluated from within its own paradigm. However, as we argue in Section 3.3, this new boldness in theology should not be confused with domination. The most striking example of giving in to this latter temptation is given by John Milbank: 'unless other disciplines are (at least implicitly) ordered to theology . . . they are objectively and demonstrably null and void, altogether lacking in truth'.[53] Notice how this is but the mirror image of Jefferson's border cops. McCutcheon thinks that theology attempts to be science but fails in the attempt; it's a shoddy imitation. Milbank thinks all science is a bad imitation of theology.

3.1 'Science' as Modernity's Border Cop

The causes and character of modernity have been a much-debated topic in late-twentieth-century theology. Some point to Duns Scotus, others to the Reformation, some to the American founding, and the list goes on. We think that Louis Dupré is on the right track: 'modernity has reached us in waves'.[54] One significant wave portending theology's modern fate was Rene Descartes' foundationalist solution. But a solution to *what*? Dupré cites Descartes' foundationalism as primarily 'overcoming the scepticism that has resulted from the nominalist crisis'.[55] This may be right but it strikes us as needlessly over-intellectualizing. Put more simply, if all of Europe disagrees about what political and human life is *for* – or even if it is *for* anything at all – the basis for resolving political and moral disagreement disappears, and all of Europe could descend into violence. Which is exactly what Europe did in Descartes' time, for thirty plus years.

Descartes and the rest of the boys in the band – Hume, Kant, Mill – each had their own spin on the solution. How to resolve moral, political and epistemological disagreements in a situation of reasonable pluralism? Perhaps no one put the problem more evocatively than John Locke:

---

[52] McCutcheon 2005, 19.   [53] Milbank 2000, 45.   [54] Dupré 2008, 3.   [55] Dupré 2008, 3.

The mind has a different relish, as well as the palate; and you will as fruitlessly endeavour to delight all men with riches or glory ... as you would to satisfy all men's hunger with cheese or lobsters; though very agreeable and delicious fare to some, are to others extremely nauseous and offensive ... Hence it was, I think, that the philosophers of old did in vain inquire, whether *summum bonum* consisted in riches, or bodily delights, or virtue, or contemplation: they might have as reasonably disputed, whether the best relish were to be found in apples, plums, or nuts, and have divided themselves into sects upon it.[56]

The question of religious disagreement and pluralism has not disappeared. See Kirk Lougheed's work on whether there are empirically informed solutions to these issues.[57]

If the *summum bonum* amounts to a taste preference – Lobster or cheese? Luther or Zwingli? Friendship or fornication? – then Christian natural law lacks the power to guide us to our own happiness. One way to diagnose modern theology's crisis is as a series of failed attempts to meet this challenge; a way to keep natural law working in the face of pluralism.

An increasingly ideological generation of thinkers turned this quest for certainty into a movement for emancipation. Dupré mentions Voltaire and Gibbon, but the theme of liberation is widespread. For example, here's Thomas Jefferson:

may it be to the world ... the signal of arousing men to burst the chains under which monkish ignorance and superstition had persuaded them to bind themselves ... The general spread of the light of science has already laid open to every view the palpable truth, that the mass of mankind has not been born with saddles on their backs.[58]

Of course, the irony of this statement was lost on Jefferson because, in his mind, there were exceptions. Some people – namely, Africans – *were* born predestined by race to wear saddles on their backs and Jefferson thought he had the science to prove it.[59] We can see how the ciphers of 'religion' and 'science' are being used not only to signal epistemic polarities of ignorance and insight, but political ideas of slavery and freedom.

When figures like Draper and White are read as late and minor characters within this larger narrative, we can better see what they were up to. They were two of many who joined Descartes and Locke on their quest for certainty and joined Voltaire and Jefferson on their quest for emancipation. They *created* something they called 'science' that was good, and something called 'religion' that was bad. Our interest, theologically speaking, is what all these figures

---

[56] Locke 1975, 2:21.56.   [57] Lougheed 2021.   [58] Jefferson 1826.   [59] Mendenhall 2013.

share; namely, advocating for a universal and neutral criterion that could sort the rational wheat from the superstitious chaff. If deductive certainty or subjective taste preferences are the only options, into which box do theological and ethical claims fit? It was never clear. William Wood labels those who would exclude theology and ethics from the rational discourse of public institutions, such as universities, the field's 'border cop'.[60]

The intellectual descendants of these Enlightenment border cops are still with us. One well-known example is Russell McCutcheon, who not only lets in scholars with a so-called view from nowhere – Jefferson's science – but has begun permitting academic work that critiques relations of power, sex, politics, class and race (i.e., uses the methods of critical theory).[61] This, finally, is something different from modernity's standard policing strategy and it bodes well for theology. However, by playing this card, McCutcheon gives up on his sorting mechanism, which sought to exclude the (so called) non-scientific study of religion. Why so? Because *plenty* of confessional theologians use the tools of critical theory to address such power relations. In fact, McCutcheon's 2013 article is ostensibly about how he wants to allow in all deconstructing critiques of religion *but not Karl Barth's*. (His reason? Because, 'science!') The argument is, shall we say, strained.

> *Sometimes a well-established discovery in a particular scientific field throws up a genuine problem for a particular interpretation of some doctrine; these localized conflicts are not to be glossed over as inconvenient but incorporated into theological argumentation. An example of this can be seen in Daniel Pedersen's use of the idea of evolved dispositions, and examples of chimpanzee killings, to question the justice of damnation.[62]*

Where we agree with McCutcheon is in his attempt to say that academics should make themselves open to challenges from all sorts of quarters, especially (but not exclusively) those concerning relations of power, politics, class, race and gender.[63] But McCutcheon appears only willing to learn from religion provided that *theology has learnt its lesson* and now plays by science's rules. Beyond mere inconsistency, this argument boils down to refusing to learn from the sources that disrupt the status quo: the modern capitalist order, or the feudal order, or bureaucratic management structures or – seemingly closest to McCutcheon's heart – the liberal rationalist order. Put another way, ironically,

---

[60] Wood 2017.
[61] McCutcheon 2013. Also, see the considerable online discussion surrounding McCutcheon 1997.
[62] Pedersen 2021.
[63] We add *not exclusively* because theories of race, gender, and so on, can themselves sometimes entrench rather than liberate.

McCutcheon's sort of science is conservative and can be imperialistic or colonialist. Our preferred phrasing would be, theology, like the sciences, is *not* committed to being a good law-abiding citizen.[64] Sometimes theology stirs up the reigning order – like it did in the British evangelical abolitionist movement over (need it be added) scientific objections that held that the races were fundamentally unequal. Sometimes it's science that stirs things up – like findings that challenge gender binarism over (need it be added) theological objections to the contrary. Scholars need not abandon commitments to creed or tradition, but they must be willing to challenge, and be challenged by, prevailing assumptions.

3.2 Throwing the Furniture Around: Theology's New Boldness

What were theologians up to amidst the border cops' battles? For the most part, the church played defence by affecting a relation of harmony. Theologians of different traditions did so in different ways. The theologically conservative agreed to play the foundationalism game and doubled-down that the Bible could provide deductively certain, universal and neutral knowledge, from which we get the doctrine of inerrancy.[65] The theologically liberal refused the game and, mostly via Kant and Schleiermacher, forced theology to seem more *wissenschaftlich* by (oddly enough) retreating into the private sphere of subjective religious feelings.[66] Written the same decade as Draper's book, Charles Hodge captures those two options, making clear his own preference for the former:

> The duty of the Christian theologian is to ascertain, collect, and combine all the facts which God has revealed in the Bible ... It may be admitted that the truths which the theologian has to reduce to a science ... are revealed partly in the external works of God, partly in the constitution of our nature, and partly in the religious experience of believers; yet lest we should err in our inferences from the works of God, we have a clearer revelation of all that nature reveals, in his word; and lest we should misinterpret our own consciousness and the laws of our nature, everything that can be legitimately learned from that source will be found recognized and authenticated in the Scriptures ...[67]

By asserting that 'all the facts' are knowable from an inerrant Bible, Hodge thought he was sticking to his guns, not retreating. However, seen in the context of the nineteenth-century university both paths were defensive manoeuvres.

One young Swiss theologian had a decidedly different take. Seeing the subsequent years as a 'period of deep shadow'[68] for theology, Karl Barth rejected the premise: Schleiermacher's and Hodge's options were not the only

---

[64] McCormack 2008, 289.   [65] Murphy 1996, 6.   [66] Tonstad 2020, 498.
[67] Hodge 1871, 1:11.   [68] Barth 1961, 19.

choices. Theology could still be real theology, in fact it could *only* be theology, by choosing none of the above. The problem with this aspect of the Barthian revolt was, ironically, what endeared Barth to so many. By so forcefully saying *Nein!* to the leading contenders of the age, he left himself less room for his alternative.[69] As the novelist Flannery O'Connor said by way of praise, 'I distrust folks who have ugly things to say about Karl Barth. I like old Barth. He throws the furniture around'.[70]

Barth wasn't only throwing furniture; he was pointing to a different kind of theology. But O'Connor was right. A third way between modernity's options would have to be *extracted* from Barth's vision, rather than following directly from it. In this section and the next, we trace two of these theological movements that followed Barth out of the cul-de-sac of modernity: the Yale school, postliberalism associated with George Lindbeck and Stanley Hauerwas, and the Radical Orthodoxy of John Milbank.

George Lindbeck's career became so associated with the founding of postliberal, Yale school theology, we sometimes forget where he started. Together with his colleague, Hans Frei – who was the premier interpreter of Barth for the American audience – Lindbeck's *Nature of Doctrine* was written to make sense of doctrinal change in the ecumenical movements of the 1980s. Lindbeck and Frei endeavoured to carve a middle path between the conservative focus on doctrinal truth and the liberal non-cognitive view of human spirituality. Drawing on Clifford Geertz and building on the linguistic turn in philosophy, Lindbeck labelled the conservative position *cognitive-propositional* and the liberal view, *experiential-expressive*.

The Nature of Doctrine succeeded in *naming*, in a theoretical way, the theological cul-de-sacs of modernity (Hodge's and Schleiermacher's, as we have been calling them). Lindbeck's third way was called the *cultural-linguistic* model. Theological knowledge is locally situated in the biblical narrative because *all* knowledge is situated in – take your pick – paradigms, traditions, practices, language games, and cultures. The only way to validate doctrinal statements is intratextually, from within a culturally specific system of signs and meanings. Not only was the foundationalist quest for certainty a sham and always bound to fail, theology can now be seen as on par with other sciences, which are similarly embedded within their own paradigms. Theology can speak

---

[69] Barth's *Nein!* (1934) was not just a rejection of Emil Brunner's idea that a formal image of God is retained after the Fall. Barth's (bizarrely) strong stance on this question can only be understood when seen as a symptom of his broader rejection of liberal theology, which presupposes that humanity has natural resources to prepare it to receive the Gospel. This, Barth worried, allows idolatrous patterns of human thinking to condition the interpretation of God self-revelation.

[70] O'Conner 1986, 180–1.

with a newly recovered confidence and has room to accept the findings of other sciences, which are no longer a threat. As Kathryn Tanner once put it, this is theology's 'new boldness'.[71]

The theological ethicist, Stanley Hauerwas, took this insight further. 'In his reception of postliberalism, Hauerwas ... added a flavor of cultural crisis to the discourse on postliberal theology, implying that intratextuality could be taken more ontologically as a way to propose an alternative social vision for theology (compared to the liberal and secular vision that permeated liberal theology)'.[72] Even the first few pages of *Resident Aliens*, Hauerwas's most-read book, are enough to show how he advances the trajectory of Barth, Lindbeck and Frei. Hauerwas and co-author William Willimon relate the following anecdote:

> One of our former parishes was next door to the synagogue. One day over coffee, the rabbi remarked, "it's tough to be a Jew in Greenville. We are forever telling our children, 'that's fine for everyone else, but it's not fine for you. You are special. You are different. You are a Jew. You have a different story. A different set of values.'"
>
> 'Rabbi, you are probably not going to believe this', I said, 'but I heard very much that same statement made in a young couples' church school class right here in Bible-belt Greenville the other day.' ... And we believe that recognition signals a seismic shift in the world view of our church, which makes all the difference in the world for how we go about the business of being the church.

An example of using psychology to help develop ecclesial ethics and practices is given by Brittany Tausen's and Katherine Douglass's work on how the tools of social-cognitive psychology inform spiritual formation practices?[73]

Here Hauerwas extends Lindbeck's grammatical metaphor of Christian doctrine, which conceived of theological claims being comprehensible only within a language, into something more. According to the anecdote, like diaspora Jews living as resident aliens in Babylon (or South Carolina), Christians not only have a distinctive language, but the church has its own culture, ethics, politics, culinary practices and even, according to Tanner, its own geography.[74] What Hauerwas adds to the previous postliberalism is an element of countercultural politics. For Hauerwas, the church must resist the existing liberal order, with its false dogmas of separation of church and state, capitalism and inalienable rights.

Lindbeck, Hauerwas and others around this time placed theology on an equal footing with other disciplines by emphasizing that all knowledge exists within

---

[71] Tanner 2010, 39.   [72] Martinson 2013.   [73] Tausen and Douglass 2021.
[74] Tanner 1997, 99.

paradigms, traditions or frameworks. One can see this idea ripple across many aspects of academia in the late twentieth century, from Rudolf Carnap's principle of semantic toleration, to Kuhn's paradigms in natural science (see Section 4.2), to Alasdair MacIntyre's traditions of ethical discourse. The shared insight is that the criteria for evaluating truth claims or ethical actions, for determining appropriate methods and practices, is tradition-specific. The most powerful critiques are those that come from within, rather than from some fanciful position of neutrality.

Before we get to the second post-Barthian response to modernity, we need to head off two objections that are especially relevant to using their thought for a science-engaged theology: George Lindbeck's alleged relativism and Stanley Hauerwas' alleged sectarianism.

Lindbeck had sought to clarify his position via what has become a 'somewhat notorious' illustration.[75] 'The crusader's battle cry "*Christus est Dominus*," for example, is false when used to authorize cleaving the skull of the infidel (even though the same words in other contexts may be a true utterance). When thus employed, it contradicts the Christian understanding of Lordship as embodying, for example, suffering servanthood'.[76] Some interpreters worry that Lindbeck is downgrading the truth value of doctrinal claims.

If *Christus est Dominus* is a false utterance *because* of what the crusader has in his 'heart', it appears that truth is *less than* correspondence. This worry is parallel to what some philosophers of science have said about Thomas Kuhn's paradigms (see Section 4.3). We suspect that much of this line of attack is rooted in a conflation of all non-foundationalist epistemologies with the extravagances of someone like Richard Rorty. In fact, Lindbeck's view of truth is far from Rorty's. The crusader's words are indeed false, but not because Lindbeck thinks that truth can be less than correspondence. He thinks he is *upgrading* truth over the cognitive-propositional view that dominated conservative Protestant wings of the church throughout late modernity (e.g., Hodge's). As Kevin Vanhoozer once put it, metaphors 'are not susceptible to literal paraphrase, not because they are noncognitive but because they have a *surplus* of cognition'.[77] Therefore, we judge that postliberal theology succeeds in pointing a way for theology's new boldness without giving into the worry of relativism.

We can easily see why Hauerwas raises similar concerns. He declines to provide publicly accessible reasons for why Christians do and say the things they do, as the rabbi struggled to explain it to the Jewish youth of Greenville – apart from saying, 'you are different'. Why are public reasons so important? If

---

[75] Lindbeck 1989, 403.   [76] Lindbeck 1984, 64.   [77] Vanhoozer 2005, 88.

Christians themselves are convinced by the gospels and Jews by the Torah, isn't that enough? Hauerwas's primary critics in this regard have been Jeffery Stout and, Hauerwas's own doctoral supervisor, James Gustafson.[78]

Gustafson's worry is that Hauerwas's theology is *Wittengensteinian fideism*. For such theologies, Gustafson argues, 'there are various language games in culture: scientific, religious, aesthetic and moral. Among these it is clear that the language of science and the language of religion (including theology) are totally incommensurable. The language of religion is therefore exempt from critical assessment from any scientific perspective; it is free from criticism from all perspectives other than its Own'.[79] If Christian theology is untouchable from other disciplines, if it exists in an intellectual ghetto, then Gustafson fears it 'isolates Christianity from taking seriously the wider world of science and culture and limits the participation of Christians in the ambiguities of moral and social life in the patterns of interdependence in the world'.[80] The heart of this worry is not that Hauerwas downgrades truth, which perhaps would be understandable: if everything is true (within its own game), perhaps nothing is true. No, the real concern is that Christians will have no way to self-correct our own traditions or settle disagreements internal to the church.

Here we return to our own 'somewhat notorious' example from Section 1.1.3. The Roman Catholic Church teaches that 'gluten-free [breads] are invalid matter for the celebration of the Eucharist'.[81] To a real Wittengensteinian fideist, this statement operates solely within the religious language game, so the key terms – Eucharist, invalid, bread and even gluten – can be defined however the Church wants. But the pope isn't a Wittengensteinian fideist. Is Hauerwas himself guilty of such thinking? No. In his response to Gustafson, Hauerwas says explicitly: 'I have avoided all appeals to a Kuhnian-like position [which is] ... designed to protect theological conviction from possible scientific challenge'. Instead, Hauerwas – and here we agree – suggests that rather than granting 'science qua science an overriding veridical status', we should 'indicate which scientific conclusions should be considered and why'.[82] We need to be specific and consider the implications of each scientific theory, study or discovery for theology on a case-by-case basis.

---

[78] Stout 2004; Gustafson 2013.   [79] Gustafson 2013, 85.   [80] Gustafson 2013, 84.

[81] Ratzinger clarifies, 'Low-gluten hosts (partially gluten-free) are valid' (2003).

[82] Hauerwas 2001, 98–9. It is intriguing to note, however, that by using the example science within his broader argument for the rationality and public accountability of Christian ethics in liberal society, Hauerwas is reinforcing Jefferson's use of 'science' as a proxy for rationality and emancipation. Maybe Alasdair MacIntyre does something similar at the beginning of *After Virtue*.

3.3 The Supreme Empress of the Sciences?

John Milbank, speaking for the perspective known as Radical Orthodoxy, has
a different version of how theology can best relate to other fields of inquiry. Like
Barth, Milbank sees that there is no neutral ground or view from nowhere. As he
opens his influential *Theology and Social Theory*, 'Once, there was no
"secular"'.[83] All knowledge is situated within paradigms, or as Milbank says,
are 'traditioned reason' that cannot be abstracted 'from the specificity of time
and place'.[84] Thus far, we can recognize how Milbank has influenced our own
thinking, as he influenced Peter Harrison, and why he deserves his place
alongside other post-Barthian movements that have given new confidence to
theologians working in secular universities.

However, Radical Orthodoxy takes this logic a step too far. John Milbank's
boldness often morphs into an audacity that claims theology should dominate
other disciplines, rather than receive the wisdom they have to offer. In the end,
this only creates a new myth of conflict. Milbank's conflict is not between
science and religion, but between what he describes as competing theologies.
Milbank takes the argument that all reasoning is traditioned a step further than
the earlier postliberals (or us) by claiming that if the other sciences do not
acknowledge that the world and our ways of knowing participate in God, then
they are meaningless. We might say that Milbank has swapped out the Logical
Positivists verificationism (theology is meaningless; see Section 4.2) for his
own Platonic participationism (everything *except* theology is meaningless).

After modernity, Milbank writes, 'theology, in the face of secular attack, is
only on secure ground if it adopts the most extreme mode of counterattack:
namely that unless other disciplines are (at least implicitly) ordered to
theology … they are objectively and demonstrably null and void, altogether
lacking in truth'.[85] But what would it look like *in practice* to order other
disciplines to theology? What does 'demonstrably null and void' imply about,
say, a particular theory in biology or sociology? Demonstrably by whom? We
could even go all the way down this path, and establish Departments of
Christian Mathematics, a possibility that Milbank raises – jokingly, we think.[86]

What is Milbank's solution to the problem that modernity created for theology? The last section of *Theology and Social Theory* begins with 'an assertion: of theology as itself a social science, and the queen of the sciences for the
inhabitants of the *altera civitas*, on pilgrimage through this temporary world'.[87]
It is critical that theology take up its place as queen of the sciences, Milbank

---

[83] Milbank 2006, 9.   [84] Milbank 2000, 55.   [85] Milbank 2000, 45.   [86] Milbank 2006, 380.
[87] Milbank 2006, 380.

argues, but not just for inhabitants of the city of God; all other disciplines quite literally depend upon it.

Note that very (very) few figures in the Christian tradition refer to theology as the queen of the sciences. It too is a much-told myth, a slice of revisionist history. Of late, the scholars who refer to theology as queen have been quick to add, *Oh, but not the bad sort of queen*. Not like 'Boadicea, Queen Victoria, and the like' (says Gavin D'Costa), 'not a high-handed dominatrix' (John Webster), 'only a "queen" of the sciences if humility determines her work' (Hauerwas).[88] If you find yourself clarifying your metaphors so often, maybe find another metaphor.

Our problem is not with the hierarchic relations conveyed by the metaphor. Neither is our problem with the asymmetry. Nor indeed is our problem with saying theology studies a more excellent object than other fields, as unfashionable as it feels to say this out loud. We agree with Thomas that theology is the noblest in some respects. If, *ex hypothesi*, it so happens that one of the sciences concerns the happiness of all humans and the flourishing of non-human animals, the planet and the cosmos, that science *would* be noble. No, our problem with theology being 'queen' is that it's not a part of the historic Christian tradition and, no one, it seems, has a solid understanding of what it would mean, even if it were.

The earliest recorded source that refers to theology by the exact phrase *regina scientiarum* seems to be from Galileo – more on this shortly. Other than a throwaway line from Erasmus's notes, we get the language most immediately from Immanuel Kant, but he gave the crown to metaphysics.[89] As far as we have found, the first writer to use a variant of the phrase is Philo, for whom queen of the sciences (βασιλίδα τών επιστημών) was astronomy.[90] The first Christian writer to use the regal metaphor appears to be Clement of Alexandria, when he says, 'wisdom is therefore queen [κυρία] of philosophy', which is closer, but nowadays this is a minority translation.[91]

Galileo turns out to be one of the few writers who takes a step back and asks, what does it mean to say that theology (or any discipline) is queen of the sciences? Like us, Galileo suspects some 'equivocation in failing to specify the virtues which entitle sacred theology to the title of "queen"'.[92] He contrasts two main options for interpreting this metaphor. The first interpretation holds

---

[88] Hauerwas 2007, 31; D'Costa 2011; Webster 2011, 59. Thanks to Sarah Lane Ritchie for pointing us in the direction of the Webster quote.

[89] Zakai 2007, 126.   [90] Runia 1986, 226.

[91] Clement of Alexandria 1991, book 1. More recent translations have 'wisdom is in authority over philosophy'. Presumably if Clement meant queen in the sense which concerns us here, he would have written βασιλίδα like Philo did. Thanks to Oliver Langworthy for pointing this out.

[92] Galilei 1957, 192.

that a queenly discipline is one that includes all knowledge that is also learnt in other disciplines, but the queen alone has better methods. Imagine, he says, that both theology and geometry can tell you the area of a circle, theology by direct inspiration from God and geometry from careful study. If theology being queen means that, 'these others must rather be referred to her [theology] as their supreme empress, changing and altering their conclusions according to her statutes and decrees', Galileo concludes that this meaning 'will not be affirmed by theologians who have any skill in the other sciences'. He knows full well that any scientist priest will not turn to the Bible for help with geometry; he will, and should, read Euclid. If theology was such a queen, she would be 'an absolute despot', who without having trained in medicine or architecture, undertakes 'to administer medicines and erect buildings according to his whim – at grave peril of his poor patients' lives, and the speedy collapse of his edifices'.[93]

According to the second interpretation offered by Galileo, a queenly discipline studies 'a subject which excels in dignity all the subjects which compose the sciences, and because her teachings are divulged in more sublime ways'. This was Galileo's preferred interpretation, and it is also quite close to the answer Thomas gives to the first question of the *Summa*. Thomas doesn't say anything about a queen, of course, but he does say that theology is the noblest discipline. Why? His reason is that it studies the worthiest subject matter (God), is directed towards humanity's true purpose and proper end (*aeterna beatitudo*) and is the most certain science (by revelation).[94]

The consistent teaching of the church has been that 'other sciences are called the handmaidens [*ancillae*; literally, household servants] of' theology, which, we guess, could maybe imply theology's position as a noblewoman, but not necessarily a queen.[95] We assume this is what Milbank and countless others – including us in a previous article[96] – had in mind when they perpetuate the myth that 'everyone' used to say that theology is the queen of the sciences. Bonaventure gives perhaps the most thorough analysis of theology's relationship to other disciplines in the medieval period, though even he does not use the

---

[93] Galilei 1957, 193.

[94] Allow us to head off a minor but oft-told myth: 'What we call "theology," Aquinas called "holy teaching" (*sacra doctrina*) ... It was *sacra doctrina*, not *theologia*, that Aquinas called a *scientia*' (Soskice 2022, 144). In fact, Aquinas called *both* sciences and, sometimes, used the terms interchangeably, which was common practice for much of Christian history. It was Augustine, not Aquinas, who was more concerned with distinguishing his faith seeking understanding from θεολογία, presumably because of its use in Varro and Plato.

[95] The closest Thomas ever gets to queenly language is when he writes, 'the ultimate goal of philosophy is beneath that of theology and ordered to it, theology ought to rule (*imperare*) all the other sciences and to make use of what is taught in them'. Aquinas 1929, q.1 a.1. See also McGinn 2008, 817.

[96] Perry and Leidenhag 2021.

metaphor.[97] What Bonaventure does say is very close to the view we are proposing in this Element. Namely, that 'all branches of knowledge serve theology, and therefore she takes illustrations and uses terms pertaining to every kind of knowledge'.[98]

For Thomas, Bonaventure, Clement and, much later, John Henry Newman, the heart of the handmaiden metaphor is that *theology needs the help of others to do its job*. Theology is on the hook, as it were, to do great and purposeful things, but because human intelligence 'is more easily led by what is known through natural reason', theology cannot do its job without other disciplines.[99] Thomas's examples here all speak of a dependent relationship between the sciences. 'Just as the musician accepts on authority the principles taught him by the mathematician', as the science of perspective depends on geometry, and as political science needs military science (because 'the good of the army is directed to the good of the state', not the other way round), so also is theology related to other fields of inquiry.[100]

Kathryn Tanner provides a more recent version of Thomas' argument. Tanner speaks of the 'both exalted and, at the same time, lowly' vocation of theology.[101] Theology seeks to be 'comprehensive' and 'exempt no element or aspect of the universe from theological comment'.[102] Yet, 'theology does not try to insure this comprehensiveness by generating out of its own resources all there is to say on these matters'.[103] Tanner is worth quoting at length, not least because of her use of different metaphors than the queen trope.

> The theologian who produces a comprehensive commentary is, therefore, not like a self-determined creator of cultural artifacts – say, a writer of a novel or a composer of a symphony. He or she is, instead, like an active reader or an orchestra conductor metaphorizing the artistic creation of others, diverting it from its intended course, transposing it into a new register or key. When producing a comprehensive commentary, the theologian does not provide his or her own place of habitation. The theologian engaged in such an enterprise is, instead, a perpetual renter, making do, making use of, working over the property of other disciplines, in the service of theology's own interests and purposes. The theologian producing a comprehensive commentary is, poor and incapacitated, a poacher or a parasite. Like those birds that lay their eggs only in other birds' nests, theologians bring their hope for a comprehensive commentary to fruition only by interjecting their own distinctive viewpoint within the space of other disciplines.[104]

Like the queen, these metaphors are not perfect. With Hauerwas we want to retain that theology does have a habitation of its own to return to, the church, and a language to speak or key to sing in. And yet, when a theologian seeks to provide a comprehensive commentary on human life or creation, she needs all the tools and best insights that the wider academy can offer.

We think that this should be enough to express the sort of dependence relationship that the Christian tradition maintains.[105] In case more is needed, Clement makes his use of the metaphor unambiguous. He renders the analogate, household servant, as *handmaiden*, of which Hagar is the archetype: 'Sarah having no child, assigned her maid, by name Hagar, the Egyptian, to Abraham, in order to get children. Wisdom, therefore, who dwells with the man of faith . . . was still barren and without child in that generation'.[106] So in Clement, wisdom or theology needs other sciences in order to be generative, to do its job, as Abraham and Sarah needed Hagar. It is not even in view that Sarah is somehow made a queen through all of this, whatever we now make of the more abusive aspects of the original story.

Now that we have surveyed something of the (largely absent) history, what type of queen does Milbank have in mind when he gives his grand 'assertion: of theology as itself a social science, and the queen of the sciences'? Milbank is closer to Galileo's first interpretation: theology is not only a queen, but a supreme empress. The problem with such views is best summarized by Linn Marie Tonstad. Tonstad does not want to sacrifice the bold and prophetic voice of theology to a liberal accommodationism but worries that Milbank's methods – his attempt to regain theology's place as queen – tend towards authoritarianism. One clue of this authoritarianism is that Milbank cannot account for, nor abide, diversity *within* theology.

Tonstad points out that although Milbank's theology submits 'devotionally to the judgement of God, he nonetheless retains a God-like capacity in relation to the neighbour' – or the neighbouring sciences.[107] For example, Milbank can pronounce that 'other disciplines . . . [are] about nothing whatsoever'.[108] This is why he needs to portray a unitive theology, nostalgic for Christendom, cannot admit theology's past and present moral failures, and doesn't abide 'less aggressively certain Christianities'.[109] Such nostalgia is not only a problem for Milbank, John Webster's 'theological theology', perhaps the leading post-Barthian alternative to Radical Orthodoxy, sometimes betrays a similar trend, according to Tonstad. Tonstad concludes that rather than merely claiming to be the only truly humble form of unmastery in the university, theology must 'structure itself and its relations to other disciplines in ways that actually

---

[105] Thomas' relationships of dependence shouldn't be confused with the microreductionism advocated by Putnam and Oppenheim, outlined in Section 4.2.
[106] Clement of Alexandria 1991, book 5.   [107] Tonstad 2020, 503.   [108] Milbank 2000, 41.
[109] Tonstad 2020, 502.

embody' repentance for past failings. Namely, for theology to engage the other sciences as a resource for self-critique, and as Bonaventure taught, as a source for theological insight.

Milbank and Webster *should* be well-positioned to learn from diverse sources in precisely the way that Tonstad and us propose. When Milbank describes, Christianity as 'the *sociality* of harmonious difference' – we couldn't agree more. But where Milbank then writes 'it is so important to reassert theology as a master discourse', we argue that harmony requires teachability.[110] Milbank, and to a lesser extent Webster, sometimes fail to acknowledge is that theology has spoken, at times, for a deeply unjust tradition and only with the aid of hand-maidens has theology been able to learn to continually repent of this injustice.[111] Christian theologians have often taken common terms and subverted them, often with countercultural effect: 'Lord', 'love' and 'person' come to mind.[112] Perhaps something similar can be done with 'queen' – but if such subversion is to be genuine then it must be accompanied by a sincere repentance for past mistakes, present limitations and continual dependency on a wide range of sources.

We do not want to swing the pendulum back to where it was before Barth. There are more options than a theology that is either a serf or a queen. What such a conflict driven picture misses is the essentially porous nature of university faculties, including the faculty of theology. Theologians trained and teaching in university settings 'depend heavily on insights from other disciplines in order to do their work', just as academics housed in other departments frequently draw upon, and may need to presuppose, theological ideas; 'theologians work *inside* the university, without the possibility of clearly separating its practices from their own'.[113] The boundaries between natural science and theology are already more porous than many have acknowledged, especially those who are engaged in a perceived struggle for either a true modern foundation like McCutcheon's border cop or a postmodern master-narrative like Milbank's queen.

3.4 Conclusion

In this section, we evaluated the totalizing narratives that come from Jefferson's descendants (external to theology) and Barth's descendants (internal to theology). In short, McCutcheon thinks that all theology is bad science, and Milbank thinks that all science is bad theology. But some of Barth's other descendants, namely, the Yale School or postliberal theology, are more successful in the efforts to defend theology's place in the university while retaining its bold, prophetic voice. If we are to avoid relativism and sectarianism, theology

---

[110] Milbank 2006, 5–6. [111] Tonstad 2020, 498.
[112] Thanks to an anonymous reviewer for this insight. [113] Tonstad 2020, 505.

must claim that the Christian truth is the only truth, and it applies to everybody. Yet the Christian truth is not the same as any one theologian's theology. If we need evidence for such a distinction, we need look no further than the abuse and injustice that characterises so much church history. Theology needs the help of other disciplines to speak truly of God and all things in relation to God.

4 Unity and Pluralism in Science

4.1 From a Great Empire to Small Allotments – and Back Again

We've seen that the term 'science' doesn't mean the same thing in all times and places, and it has sometimes served as a proxy for emancipation, rationality and progress – or a characteristically modernist version of these. What, then, is it that science-engaged theologians are meant to engage *with*? Here, we have in mind something narrower; the subset of academic disciplines which investigate the world with empirical tools, especially since the Scientific Revolution. But even science in this narrower sense has its own controversy and backstory. Telling this story, or at least selected episodes from it, is the purpose of this section.

Before that, a word about where we are headed. As we will see shortly, there have been many attempts to unify the various scientific disciplines and methods into 'one thing'. None of these attempts have worked, and the effort is often politically motivated. Instead, we can embrace the disunity of the sciences. Doing so is good for theology because it forces theologians engaging with the sciences to stay local and specific. Not only does specificity allow for the kind of deep engagement that can shed genuinely novel insights on theological questions, but it also facilitates more equal interpersonal collaborations that lie at the heart of contemporary university research culture.

In the 1830s, after the decline of natural philosophy – which had held science together as *scientia*, the sum of the liberal arts – William Whewell bemoaned what was lost along the way.

> Formerly, the learned embraced in their wide grasp all the branches of the tree of knowledge ... But these days are past; the students of books and of things are estranged from each other in habit and feeling. But the disintegration goes on, like that of a great empire falling to pieces; physical science itself is endlessly subdivided, and the subdivisions insulated ... And thus science, even mere physical science, loses all traces of unity ... The inconveniences of this division of the soil of science into infinitely small allotments have been often felt and complained of.

This 'evil', as Whewell called it, was partly caused by the lack of 'any name by which we can designate the students of the knowledge of the material world collectively'. He solved that problem by proposing a list of possible labels for the new profession. One from his list that he felt was 'not generally palatable' was the word, *scientist*.[114] It caught on nevertheless.

Fast forward one century. In the 1930s, long after the term proved more successful than Whewell could have hoped, some detected signs that the pendulum had swung too far. Philosopher Edgar Brightman – remembered today as the mentor of Martin Luther King, Jr – wrote of the consequences of this unification. Instead of 'infinitely small allotments', Brightman faced a too great empire: 'to derive a concept of verification from one field and to clamp it down on all fields is, even when baptized by the sacred name of scientific method, not method, but methodological dogmatism ... A mathematician verifies his results by one type of procedure, a physicist by another, an historian by another'.[115] The very fact that Brightman had to argue for this was a sign of how much had changed since the 1830s. What should have been relevant differences between disciplines were elided or flattened out. Brightman was trying to counteract the myth that, seeing as they were all *scientists*, they were subject to the same methods, be they biologists, historians, anthropologists and so on.

Much of the work relevant to our question in this section – in science-engaged theology, what is theology meant to engage *with* – oscillates between these poles. Nowadays, outside the confines of philosophy of science journals, we appear to have gone too far towards Whewell's empire. We don't think anything is strange with the question, 'What does science think about that?' or the statement, 'Science teaches us that ...', but we should. There is more than one type of unity and in what follows we look at various misguided attempts to unify the sciences.

4.2 The Unifiers

Whewell's proposal for propping up the fallen empire by coining 'scientist' might seem a bit too silly to have much effect. In the same article, he reviewed Mary Somerville's 1834 best-seller, *On the Connexion of the Physical Sciences*, and he there found a less silly effort:

> If we apprehend her purpose rightly, this is to be done by showing how detached branches have, in the history of science, united by the discovery of general principles ... in the same way in which a kindred language proves the common stock and relationship of nations, the connexion of all the sciences

---

[114] Whewell 1834, 59. Whewell hoped this would carry the kind of authority associated at the time with the title 'artist', but also worried it would be more reminiscent of 'dentist' and the unfortunate need to earn a living.

[115] Brightman 1937, 149.

which are treated of in the work now before us is indicated by the community
of that mathematical language which they all employ.[116]

Her strategy of looking for unity via the conjunction of language and math
would prove prescient for the other unifiers who would shortly appear on the
scene. Here, we mention four schools of thought that sought to unify science: via
the language of laws, via logical analysis, via methodology and via reductionism.

From the start, the search for unity was indistinguishable from broader
political and social concerns. The same individuals who formed the German
School of 1847, seeking to unify human physiology in Newtonian physics, also
fought to unify Germany in the Professor's Revolution in 1848.[117] These
German liberals wanted to revolt against feudalism without provoking the
anarchy of the French Reign of Terror. Put simply, the hope to unify nature
through universally applicable natural laws was bound up with the unification of
Germany with common national laws.

An appeal to laws was not the only way to unify science. In order to know if the
laws of one science (like physiology) could be inferred from another (like
physics) we would first need a shared language. This was the kind of semantic
unity of science sought by the logical empiricists, such as Otto Neurath and
Rudolf Carnap. One way to understand the context of such a project is to consider
the following question: as Whewell's empire of natural philosophy crumbled into
the allotments of natural, human and social sciences, what was left for
philosophy?[118] It seemed like all the substantial work was being annexed. The
answer given by the logical empiricists was to focus on logic, which had recently
undergone a revolution in the work of Gottlöb Frege and Bertrand Russell.

This, in turn, led to verificationism, popularized in the English-speaking
world by A.J. Ayer, whereby synthetic statements were deemed meaningful
(capable of being either true or false) only if they could be empirically tested, at
least in principle. Statements that could be confirmed by observation or testing
could be placed in a single logical language system, giving a unity to science.
Statements, like theological and ethical claims, that could not be verified in this
way were not only unscientific, they were deemed meaningless. Carnap and
Neurath understood that for them, as for Jefferson in the eighteenth century, to
be 'scientific' was to be emancipated, to join an open realm of debate based on
evidence, to participate in a new international world order of cooperation
realized in institutions such as UNESCO and the World Health Organization.[119]

Karl Popper tried something slightly different. Rather than a shared language
for verification, Popper tried to unify the sciences with a method that could
demarcate science (e.g., Einstein's theory of relativity) from non-science

---

[116] Whewell 1834, 60.   [117] Galison 2016, 15.   [118] Creath 2021.   [119] Creath 2021.

(e.g., Marxism and Freudian psychoanalysis).[120] What worried him most was that, to Marx or Freud, every economic event or aspect of human behaviour could be interpreted to confirm their own theory. For Popper, good science is risky; it sticks its neck out, so to speak. Scientists start off with bold, imaginative conjectures, but these must then form concrete predictions that the scientist attempts to falsify. We will return to defend a version of 'riskiness' in Section 5.3.1. For now, we can say that Popper provides a clear example of how unity and demarcation (and authority) go together.

Today, by far the most common meaning of the unity of science is closer to Hilary Putnam's and Paul Oppenheim's argument that microreduction is a hypothetical ideal for all science, towards which scientist should all work.[121] Microreduction pictures the unity of science in the following way. If we want to understand why Dundee United football fans act as they do – a sociological question – we should study the psychology of, for example, Cole, one of their biggest supporters. But Cole's psychology is explained by his brain chemistry and genetics, which are neuroscientific and biological matters. However, if Cole cheers for Dundee because of his genes, what else is his DNA but fundamental particles, so really to understand Dundee United football fans comes down to physics. This picture of the sciences arises out of two convictions. First, that all you need to do to explain wholes (like the whole person) is explain the parts (the brain, the vital organs, the hormones) and once you have done that, there is nothing left to explain. The second conviction is that physics consists in discovering natural laws that determine the behaviour of all things everywhere in the universe. The result is the conclusion that if only we had a complete and perfect understanding of physics and the laws of nature, we would have a unified theory of everything. All knowledge and practical power would be within reach.

4.3 The Disunifiers

After this culmination of the hope in the unity of science, the pendulum started to swing back, away from seeing science as a great empire. Two philosophers of science were pivotal in this reversal, Mary Hesse and Thomas Kuhn. In 1961, Hesse published two books. The first, *Science and the Human Imagination* argued that 'the sciences ... have always been closely related to their cultural and religious environment'. Scientific practices not only have room 'for recognition of the transcendent' but also can be expected to change along with the

---

[120] Popper 1963, 34.

[121] Putnam and Oppenheimer 1958. Note that they reject methodological unity and semantic unity in science as 'doubtful'.

cultural and religious systems in which it is found.[122] In the same year, *Forces and Fields* argued against a single scientific method, because a wide range of criteria might justify the acceptance of a hypothesis.[123] Her most famous text, *Models and Analogies in Science* (1963) continues a more pluralistic view of scientific explanation by arguing for the eliminable role of models (not just theories) and analogy (not just deduction or inference) in scientific reasoning. Already in Hesse's work we can begin to see why pluralism might be an equalizing force in interaction between scientific and theological research.

Where Hesse's work was quietly appreciated, Thomas Kuhn's was loudly critiqued. Kuhn's *The Structure of Scientific Revolutions* (1962) argued that standards of justification, the reasons we give for thinking something to be true or false, are influenced by the larger historical, psychological, religious and sociological contexts in which an idea is produced. He thus proposed a theory of scientific change, not as an inevitable march of progress, but as rare, revolutionary 'paradigm' shifts that change the fundamental assumptions under which 'normal science' is practiced. The classic examples of this are the shift from Ptolemy's to Copernicus' solar system, and from Newtonian to Einsteinian physics. For Kuhn any two paradigms are incomparable, even 'incommensurable', because 'scientists will work in a different world' after the revolution.[124]

Kuhn did not disunify science as much as Hesse's work had started to do. He still tended to lump different disciplines together and his all-encompassing paradigms stretched hundreds of years. But both thinkers historicizing of science opened the door to a more localized approach to the question of what science is and how it works. That so many followed Hesse and Kuhn through the door labelled Disunity (or Pluralism) is probably as much to do with the timing of their publications as it is their ground-breaking arguments.

From the mid-nineteenth century until the Cold War, to speak of disunities in science was tantamount to speaking against this vision of liberal, democratic, global peace. In the 1960s and 1970s the political landscape went through its own revolution. The backlash against McCarthyism, the rise of feminism and increasing multiculturalism interpreted scientific unity as hegemonic and imperialist.[125] Today it is the disunity of science movement that champions progressive policies of protecting marginalized voices and celebrating diversity. This shift in the meaning of 'unity' is evident in the earliest dissents. In 1975, Paul Feyerabend advocated for anarchist science, because '[uniform] science that resists alternatives to the status quo' must be

---

[122] Hesse 1961b, 9–10. This is an argument revisited and extended in her final two books: Hesse 1980, 56–7; Hesse and Arbib 1987, 236–43. See Jardine 2018, 19–28.
[123] Hesse 1961a.   [124] Kuhn 1970, 121.   [125] Richardson 2006, 20.

overcome.[126] In a much-cited speech a 1978, Patrick Suppes argued that "The irreducible pluralism of languages in science is as desirable a feature as is the irreducible plurality of political views in a democracy'.[127] By 1980, the pendulum had swung back in favour of the infinitely small, specialized allotments that Whewell lamented.

So, where did philosophy of science go next? Imre Lakatos and Larry Lauden sought to moderate Kuhn's picture of scientific change by introducing the idea of simultaneous competing research programmes and traditions of inquiry. This included more competition and localized differences than Kuhn's paradigms. Others, under the heading of 'Science Studies' started to focus on how non-cognitive factors impact scientific enquiry. Still others, the so-called Stanford School, offer a daringly metaphysical version of disunity. Nancy Cartwright argues that the world is 'dappled', where physical laws work on a more regional rather than universal basis.[128] John Dupré argued against essential natural kinds because things can be accurately described and categorized for different purposes, a view he called 'promiscuous realism'. Although excitingly provocative, Cartwright's and Dupré's pluralism claims too much. There is no simple bridge from pluralism in scientific practice to a metaphysically disjunctive or promiscuous world. Instead, the most compelling form of scientific pluralism is more empirically restrained.

As characterized by Stephen Kellert, Helen Longio and C. Kenneth Waters, 'the pluralist stance' maintains that whether the world could ever, even in principle, be explained by a single, fundamental set of principles is 'an open, empirical question'.[129] Maybe the world and everything in it can be completely explained by a couple of perfect equations or laws, but maybe it cannot. In the current state of science, complete unification looks doubtful, but really, we have no way of knowing. In the meantime, scientific pluralists argue, it makes little sense to take unification to be the goal of science or the standard by which we judge all scientific methods and theories.

Rather than seeing the sciences as offering a pile of irrefutable facts about the world, we should think of scientific equipment, methods and theories as offering different perspectives on the world. Scientific perspectivism, as proposed by Ronald N. Giere, starts off with a comparison to ordinary colour vision. Most humans have three types of rods in their retina, but some have only two or even one (leading to colour blindness). Many birds have four rods, and bees even see ultraviolet. When asking 'what colour is it?' there is not just one correct answer. This irreducible diversity is not because of a metaphysically disunified world; it is because colour arises out of an *interaction* between the object and the

---

[126] Feyerabrend 1975, 39.   [127] Suppes 1993, 45.   [128] Cartwright 1999.
[129] Kellert et al. 2006, x–xiii.

observer. Different answers to the question, 'what colour is it?' can sometimes be incompatible (someone can be wrong), but they can sometimes be 'consistent and complementary' (someone can be using a different optical system). Colour perception is a real but partial perspective on the world.

What is true of ordinary visual observation, Giere argues, is also true of extended forms of observation using scientific instruments, and of theoretical perspectives. He writes, 'as an instrument may be able to record either infrared or ultraviolet, but not both, theoretical principles may deal with mechanical forces or with electromagnetic forces, but not both. Newton's equations, I would say, define a particular mechanical perspective on the world; Maxwell's equations define an electromagnetic perspective'.[130] Even Einstein's theory of special relativity, which is a more general replacement of these two, only offers a partial perspective, as shown by how it differs from the perspective of general relativity. Whether two perspectives can ever be unified, without losing information on either side, cannot be known in advance. Pluralism itself is a local rather than universal thesis.[131]

Like maps, scientific theories, models and explanations represent the world in partial and selective ways. When faced with seemingly competing alternatives, we should choose the best map for the purpose in mind. Here, 'best' depends on what type of question one is seeking to answer, what type of intervention one is hoping to achieve. This is not relativism; not all maps are equally good, but neither are they all designed for the same purpose. The London Underground map is ideal if you want to travel by subway, but not if you want to have an accurate representation of distances, depth, or just about any other information. As Mary Midgley and John Ziman write, 'scientific knowledge is incurably pluralistic ... Like geographers, scientists "map" the world in different ways for different purposes. These "maps" often overlap, yet there is no proof that they can be extended and unified into a "theory of everything" that covers all reality'.[132]

This metaphor might remind readers of the work of Peter Harrison and David Livingstone discussed in Section 2.3. We can now see more clearly what the problem is with the idea of a single map for the territories of science and religion. It's not only that, in modernity, such a map was drawn on disputed premises and with questionable motives, but that the sciences themselves consist in an almost uncountable number of different 'maps' (theories, models, explanations, methods, etc.) for understanding the natural world. Moreover, we do not have a 'master map', that explains how all the partial and limited versions fit together. The only practical response to such a situation is to continue to work at the local level, to create the best partial

---

[130] Giere 2006, 32–3.   [131] Kellert et al. 2006, xxiii.   [132] Ziman and Midgley 2001, 153.

and limited pictures of the world we can, while looking out for possible connections to the maps that others are drawing.

Bethany Sollereder explores one such 'trading-zone' in relation to the environmental crisis, and the contribution that theology can make to the science of restoration ecology.[133]

Our advice to stay local should not be confused with disciplinary isolationism or theoretical protectionism. If disunity means saying, 'psychologists should ignore biologists, and theologians ignore psychologists', then this would undermine our vision for science-engaged theology. On the contrary, the questions that most need asking and the problems that humanity faces are big complex problems. These problems require both a heightened specialization and also deep and sustained collaboration. The best way to make progress on big questions is not for one person to tackle it all at once, which leads to simplified generalizations. The benefit of 'staying local' is that it allows us to speak across disciplinary lines and set up focused trading-zones.

4.4 Speaking Pidgin in Science-Engaged Theology

The pendulum might be swinging back yet again. The philosophers that have most championed scientific plurality and disunity now acknowledge that their view resembles some aspects of Neurath's *International Encyclopedia of Unified Science*. Neurath consistently attacked his colleagues' reductionist views of unity, which supposed a common foundation of laws or sense-datum language.[134] Instead, when asked what the unifying programme of his *Encyclopedia* entailed, Neurath answered, 'the maximum of co-operation – that is the program!'[135] The purpose was not to propose a new speculative system, '*the* system of sciences', but to draw attention to the 'gaps, difficulties, and points of discussion'. As John Dewey summarizes in his entry in the *Encyclopedia*, 'it is essentially a co-operative movement, so that detailed and specific common standpoints and ideas must emerge out of the processes of co-operation'.[136]

So, what went wrong? How did Neurath get from co-operation, if that was all he really wanted, to the flawed idea of verificationism? His mistake was in thinking that 'to establish unified [co-operative] science . . . a *unified language* with a *unified syntax* is needed'.[137] The problem is, of course, different disciplines (scientific and otherwise) do not all use terms in the same way, nor do they employ the same logic or inference structures to draw conclusions. Moreover, if

---

[133] Sollereder 2021.   [134] Cat et al. 1996, 347–52.   [135] Richardson 2006, 1.
[136] Dewey 1938, 33–4.   [137] Neurath 1931/1983, 59.

the last century has taught us anything it is that we should not all be made to speak the same language or reason in the same way – such a project of translation and homogenization can only be imperialistic. This would lead to a loss of knowledge that was uniquely encapsulated in a particular community's way of speaking, reasoning and acting. If we can't rely on translation to a single *lingua franca*, how can we communicate? One unappealing option is to follow Kuhn and give up on any hope of communicating across these incommensurable paradigms. But translation and incommensurability are not the only options.

Peter Galison argues that when we look at the history of science, we see neither absolute unity with a shared single language, nor incommensurable languages lost in a sea of relativism.[138] Rather we find tireless, if halting, attempts to trade ideas and learn from one another. But without a shared system of logic, or 'semantic hygiene' as the logical empiricists sought to create, how does such collaboration work? Galison's answer comes from a project created towards the end of the Second World War:

> What happens when an H-bomb designer, a logician, an aerodynamical engineer, and a statistician sit down together? Whatever else they do, I would argue, they do not found a League of Nations with simultaneous translators (or their scientific equivalents) perched over the assemblage in metaphorical glass booths. No: they work out an intermediate language, a pidgin, that serves a local, mediating capacity. 'Randomness', 'experiment', and a host of other terms and actions coalesce into a more or less coherent sector of shared usefulness.[139]

The various sub-cultures of science coordinate their practices and theories through a series of localized unifiers and disunifiers to form overlapping (inter-digitating, Gould would say) trading zones. A 'trading zone', in Galison's words is 'an arena in which radically different activities could be *locally*, but not globally, coordinated'.[140] In such trading zones, researchers collaborate not by a neat and wholistic translation from the language of one discipline to that of another, but instead in greatly simplified pidgin languages.

To theologians of a certain generation, our endorsement of pidgin languages may sound alarm bells. To understand and respond to the two worries that theologians may have, we first need to say a bit more about three stages in the life cycle of languages, as they interact with others: pidginization, creolization and repidginization.

As linguist John Holm describes, although pidginization results from the contact of two linguistic groups, this encounter is never an equal one.[141] The more powerful group's language becomes the *superstrate* language, contributing far more than the

---

[138] Galison 1996b.   [139] Galison 1996a, 11.   [140] Galison 1996b, 119.   [141] Holm 2012, 5.

weaker *substrate*. In the creation of a pidgin, *both* languages are changed (although unequally so); vocabulary is reduced, syntax is simplified, resonances of meaning are sacrificed and understanding can be severely compromised. So far, this is not a problem. However, the worry arises when a temporary pidgin becomes a creole, which is a new fully-fledged language with native speakers who never learnt the original two languages. It should be clear why theologians might be worried about the creolization of theology and science, particularly in a context where the sciences have more social capital than the church.

> *Paul Arnold uses the interdisciplinary field of gesture studies, which includes the life-cycle of languages, to expand our understanding of liturgical and sacramental language.*[142]

Theologians like Stanley Hauerwas have given voice to this concern. Infamously, Hauerwas has opposed Christians speaking of justice.[143] Not because Christians should not care about justice, but because the only discourse with which Christians can do so with any currency is the discourse of 'human rights'.[144] While the concept of human rights may have started out as a pidgin with roots in the Christian tradition, it has now become a creole that masks the biblical understanding; justice begins with obligation to others in covenant.

Repidginization is the stage in the death of a language when there are no fluent native speakers alive any longer, but their children still use occasional terms and phrases without living in the full linguistic world of their parents. Brent Strawn has expressed concern that the Old Testament is already undergoing repidginization within the church.[145] Of course, one can imagine a different scenario where repidginization occurs because of creolization; there are no native speakers anymore because everyone is speaking the new creole. We share Hauerwas's and Strawn's concern about creolization and repidginization, but it is misplaced if it is levelled against what we are proposing for science-engaged theology.

When we describe science-engaged theology as a trading zone, and advocate theologians using a pidgin to communicate with academics from other fields, we are not imagining a total translation of theology to a lowest common denominator language, deprived of Christianity's embarrassing particularity. We are imagining using terms of particularity, temporarily abstracted from their wider linguistic framework. The key term here is *temporarily*; science-engaged

---

[142] Arnold 2022.   [143] Stout 2004, 158.

[144] Hauerwas 1999, ch. 5; 2015. For a scholar expressing a similar concern from outside Christian theology, see Mahmood 2012.

[145] Strawn 2017.

theologians must remain always ready to explain the larger picture that lies behind their concepts, as well as to listen to scientists as they explain the foreign world that lies behind seemingly familiar language. A science-engaged theologian is, in this sense, like a merchant-sailor or an explorer and not a resident alien. Even as the theologian learns more and more 'cog-sci' or 'evo-bio' lingo, and the pidgin becomes more developed, they should not forget their own native tongue, nor should they uncritically adopt aspects of 'sciencese' into their everyday speech. To that end, science-engaged theology must remain, first and foremost, 'theological theology' done by theologians who belong to ecclesial communities.[146]

Science-engaged theology should not be anyone's first language; science-engaged theology must not become creole. For this reason, we should resist the pull towards setting up a *Journal of Science-Engaged Theology* or creating undergraduate or PhD programmes in such a field.[147] Maybe in the future it will be possible to speak of 'scientific theology' (or even better, biological theology, psychological theology, geological theology) the way we speak of historical theology, philosophical theology, or eco-theology – to refer to theologians who are particularly adept and attentive to the use of the tools of historical scholarship, philosophical analysis, or ecology in their constructive work – without fears that we are somehow diluting theology or selling-out (speaking creole or a secular *lingua franca*). But we are not there yet.

4.5 Conclusion

In this section we've sided with philosophers of science who express an empirically driven agnosticism about whether there will ever be a complete and unified description of the world. This may seem surprising for two reasons. First, Christian theology has an a priori reason to affirm the (at least theoretical) unity of science, namely the unity of creation and the divine mind. But remember, we are not claiming that the world *is* disunified, metaphysically. We are making an epistemological claim; we do not know how or if the perspectives and maps of empirical enquiry fit together. And, pragmatically, it does not

---

[146] Webster 2016, 25.

[147] Galison suggests that this is what happened in his example of thermonuclear physics. 'The crude mediating language began to acquire its own journals, its own experts. By the 1960's, what had been a pidgin had become a full-fledged creole: The language of a self-supporting subculture with enough structure and interest to support research life without being an annex of another discipline, without needing translation into a "mother tongue"' (1996b, 153). Arguably, this describes the origin of fields such as 'science-and-religion' and maybe 'analytic theology', which started off as specialists clearly belonging to one field temporarily engaging with Christian theology and vice versa. However, now that science-and-religion and analytic theology have their own professorial chairs, academic journals, and masters and PhD programs, one might wonder if they have become a kind of creole.

always benefit the goals of a particular area of enquiry to prioritize such unity. One of the consequences of this pluralistic stance is that it curtails our ability to draw metaphysical conclusions from science. This is not to abandon realism, but to suggest that if one wants to do metaphysics then perhaps the tools and methods of metaphysicians should be closer to hand, rather than those of empirical scientists. Science might cast significant doubt on some metaphysical systems, but 'science itself won't answer many metaphysical questions associated with scientific inquiry'.[148] We need a theology-engaged science to help with such questions of determinism, order, intelligibility and flourishing. The result, we hope, will be a mutually enriching exchange of goods between theologians and scientists.

Second, it may seem odd for us as theologians not to join in Whewell's grief over the loss of natural philosophy, which was an empire of knowledge ordered towards God. As argued in the previous section, we do not think that the only way for theologians to speak with boldness and positively contribute to the contemporary academy is to be queen of the sciences, empress of natural philosophy, or to remember with nostalgia the bygone days of Christendom. Christendom no longer exists, and what exists on roughly the same landmass that it once did is the fragile and imperfect European Union. The EU provides something of a metaphor for our vision of the university. It is a trading zone where national boarders remain, and cultural and linguistic differences can be celebrated, but where there is also a shared set of standards allowing for increased collaboration and the relatively free movement of goods and peoples.

The discussion of the unity and plurality of the sciences might seem like a roundabout way to answer the question, 'what is this "science" that science-engaged theologians are meant to engage with?' We've provided no universal criteria for science that might demarcate it from non-science. Part of the purpose of this section has been to show why we cannot give such a clear definition. The search for such a definition presupposes that there is a quality that both unifies all the various sciences and scientific pursuits, and does not include any other pursuits (history, philosophy, theology, etc.). There is simply no such quality. Science refers to a diversity of ways to understand the world for different purposes, many features of which will partially overlap with other pursuits.

But a lack of clear borders does not make the label of science meaningless. There is still a loose grouping of empirically driven perspectives on the natural world that we might term scientific. Nor does this blurred boarder license an anything goes relativism. There are still norms to each of these various practices and explanations. There are still better and worse ways to explain the world.

---

[148] Kellert et al. 2006, xxiv.

It just does not get us very far to use the word science for all the good ways and non-science, pseudoscience, metaphysics or whatever else to describe the bad ways.

When theologians engage the sciences, they cannot engage them all at once, nor even a whole sub-discipline (biology), perhaps nor even a sub-area of sub-discipline (mood disorders). However, they must have sufficient awareness of the sub-discipline to make prudent choices about where to set up their stall, to use our metaphor of trading zones again. They will have to negotiate local customs and norms, without necessarily adopting them as norms for theology. Building such a knowledge base and, more importantly, establishing the relationships necessary for such work, may be hard and slow. Science-engaged theology is not for academic tourists.

5 The Sciences among the Sources of Theology

We have made a case for theologians, present company included, to form the habit of asking ourselves, what methods or tools could help me improve this claim we are making about the empirical world? Forming that habit, let alone successfully implementing it, is not straightforward. In the three preceding sections, we discuss some larger intellectual trends that lie behind the arrival of science-engaged theology on the scene. We also sought to clarify our vision of science-engaged theology by responding to complications that could get in the way of our recommendation to use scientific tools and findings. Some of these complications were obvious, others less so. In this section we speak more positively by presenting some of the promise and benefits of a science-engaged theology.

This section is divided into three parts, each answering an important question. First, we briefly ask, why engage the sciences in theology? Our answer is that science-engaged theology is a way for theologians to acquire virtues that help the church listen to the voice of God in the world and seek truth. Second, and perhaps most centrally, we need to know what a theological source really is, and where the sciences fit alongside theology's other sources. It turns out that sources, like academic disciplines, are not natural kinds and there is a plurality of ways to divide them up and depict their relationships. Third, how does it work in practice to use science among the other sources of theology? We start by exploring what *risky* theology might look like and explaining how the sciences can help theologians recognize when risks are appropriate. However, such a picture does not capture the rich diversity of ways that the sciences can be used as sources for theology; science-engaged theology is about more than theology sticking its neck out. It's also about searching for *entangled* concepts that take the tools of more than one discipline to understand.

5.1 Why Engage the Sciences as a Source?

We concluded Section 3 by writing of the porous nature of different fields of study. In Tonstad's words, theologians 'depend heavily on insights from other disciplines in order to do their work ... theologians work *inside* the university, without the possibility of clearly separating its practices from their own'.[149] It's almost beside the point to debate whether a given field, such as theology, engages with others; it always already does. *Almost* beside the point, but not entirely. Theology already engages other disciplines, but it does have some choice over *which* disciplines to engage at any given point. Throughout our argument, we took for granted that theologians will want to use science as a theological source – if only certain worries, some legitimate, some imagined – are overcome. We think this is a safe assumption, sociologically-speaking, but it might be objected that we haven't fully motivated the claim that theologians should engage the empirically oriented disciplines.

Given the arguments made in preceding sections, we cannot rely on scientistic assumptions regarding the superiority or unity of science. Instead, we might follow philosopher of science John Dupré, who looks for a non-question-begging way to value empirical enquiry and exclude pseudo-science. He points us in the direction of intellectual virtues. Theology's epistemic virtues will be numerous, but included in this list will surely be Dupré's 'empirical accountability', 'coherence with other things we know', and 'exposure to criticism from the widest variety of sources'.[150] Theologians have additional reasons to esteem these virtues: the conviction that God speaks through the material world and that humanity is prone to idolatry. The question is not *if* theology should engage the sciences, but how and when to do so well. These are very broad reasons for why theologians should engage with findings of particular scientific fields and studies, which by their nature will be narrow. 'But surely', our imagined interlocutor might reply, 'theology already has its own sources to help inculcate such epistemic virtues. Why does it need science too?' To answer this retort, we need to take a closer look at the sources of theology.

5.2 What are Theological Sources?

Where do theologians get their ideas? Against what criteria are doctrines evaluated? It's tempting to diffuse the question by drawing parallels to other

---

[149] Tonstad 2020, 505.   [150] Dupré 1993, 11, 243.

disciplines – chemists have the periodic table, Catholics have the catechism – but it's not that easy. When Protestant theologians debate sources, they primarily, almost exclusively, think of the so-called Wesleyan Quadrilateral, a principle articulated at the height of modernity, which claimed that doctrine should be revealed by 'Scripture, illumined by tradition, vivified in personal experience, and confirmed by reason'.[151] Some of our more erudite readers might think of Richard Hooker's tripartite system of reason, revelation, and tradition.[152] John Owen wrote, 'there is no need of Tradition ... no need of the Authority of any Churches', experience and Scripture are enough.[153] So, how many sources should we have? Wesley counted Four, Hooker counted Three, Owen counted Two and Zwingli, at points, seem to count only One.

Some interlocutors have heard us call science a source for theology and asked, 'Well, which one is it? Does science go along with reason, experience, or perhaps as a standalone fifth source?' The typical framing of the debate about theological sources, taken from early modern England, leads to this framing. Such debates are red herrings. This very idea of counting sources only leads to placing them in competition and debating which level of revelation can be reduced to another. A classic example is seen in the question, are Scripture and tradition one source or two? Since Scripture is sacred text for a particular tradition, and a tradition is sustained reflection on these particular texts, there is no clear way to answer such a question. This desire to count and order sources is characteristically modern and deeply mistaken. Theological sources are not discrete pots of information. To follow this path is to head straight back to viewing science and religion as transhistorical categories, imagining that their sources (reason and faith) are natural kinds, further entrenching the myths of Conflict and NOMA. In short, if we answer the questions 'how many sources?' and 'which pot does science go in?' in a straightforward way, we just return to the faulty map from which we started.

To avoid this fate, we need to (again!) get behind these modern debates and see that sources are not discrete pots of information, nor are the categories natural kinds. There is no objective way to count theology's sources. The same can be said for sources of scientific reflection. As Peter Godfrey-Smith reminds us,

> Empiricism is often summarized by saying that the only source of knowledge is experience. But what is this talk of 'sources' doing here? We ask, Is there just one source of knowledge, or more than one? This is like asking, is there just one pipe leading into this tank, or more than one? But the process of learning about the world is not like that; epistemology is not plumbing.[154]

[151] Wesley 2016, 103.   [152] Breward 1974.
[153] Owen 2017, 44, cited by Nuttall 1992, 43–4.   [154] Godfrey-Smith 2003, 228.

Joanna Leidenhag asks, Can contemporary embryology help elucidate how souls are inherited, as according to traducianism?[155] In investigating this, she notes how the history of medicine is deeply interwoven with theological ideas and how the second-century theologian, Tertullian, incorporated botany, as well as Scripture and tradition into his theory of the inheritance of the soul.

There are helpful parallels to be drawn between the recent discussion of the reliability of science and the religious upheavals that precipitated the English Civil War. At root, both episodes are fuelled by disagreements about authority, social power and even epistemic justice. As such, our preferred answer to the question of where science fits among the sources is to say that sometimes it is helpful to view the sciences as an extension of one particular source, sometimes as implicated in all four Wesleyan sources, and sometimes as something a bit different from any.

We must be mindful then that labelling sources of knowledge can be a power-play, and so is deciding which source best fits science. This is what was really going on in Draper's and White's narratives, where science was a proxy for forms of Christianity that prioritized rationalism. One way to interpret the invention of 'scientific creationism' or 'Genesis science' is as another, rather less successful, attempt to co-opt the power of science to champion just one source, namely Scripture. The co-option of science into an internal theological debate about which source is king has been unhelpful. To dissolve these power-plays, such as whenever theologians say, 'science is on my side', it is helpful to see how scientific practice and activity is implicated within all four of the traditional sources.

Reason is the most obvious place to start, which of course is all that is meant by medieval *scientia*. It was natural philosophy that morphed into what we call natural science. As explored in Section 3.3, *scientia* and philosophy have long been considered the handmaids of theology. But the natural sciences as we currently understand them do not neatly fit into the category of reason. Although they are a discourse based on evidence, logic, debate and intellectual discernment, they are also practices of testing, observing, measuring and recording. There is a sense in which the practices of the sciences rationalize, by narrowing, replicating and operationalizing, the theological source of experience.

Experience is often thought of as 'the runt of this epistemological litter', but not because it is weak or unpersuasive.[156] To the contrary, experience or rather 'enthusiasm' is shunned because it is too powerful. When religious experience is taken to be private, immediate and 'self-validating in an uncontestable way', then it can be used to grant unchecked power as well as to create unbridgeable divides between insiders and outsiders.[157]

---

[155] Leidenhag 2022a.   [156] Jong 2021, 483.   [157] Tanner 2010, 282.

The solution is clearly not to deny the place of experience in theological reflection. Instead, we should accept a much wider notion of experience than is portrayed in these early modern debates.[158] Experience includes the testimony of creation, the movements of providence and the political-material structures of human culture, practices of spiritual formation and liturgical participation, the intransient affects that move human bodies,[159] in addition to the secret interior movements of the Holy Spirit. Some of these forms of experience are more readily publicly available than others. But this, in the end, is no different from the highly localized and specialized experiences that give rise to scientific knowledge, which require years of training, talent and the right environmental conditions.[160] We do not want to be misunderstood; appeals to the authority of experience in theology and the contemporary sciences are not always the same kind of claims. Our point is that we cannot differentiate them, and claim legitimacy for one or the other, by simplistic appeals to a private-public or immediate-mediated divide. Furthermore, sometimes a scientific form of experience, such as an observation or an experiment, may also be a religiously significant experience.

Scientific discourse, and ever-changing groups of methods for investigation, can also be described as a tradition, as Larry Laudan argues.[161] Moreover, this empirical tradition has always been historically entangled with Christian commitments regarding the order and intelligibility of the universe, the cognitive consequences of sin and humanity's place in creation. When we present scientists as doing something theologically neutral (or secular) we can forget that the empirical sciences are a traditioned perspective for reading the natural world in a particular way.

Kimberley Kroll looks at how grafting in botany elucidates our understanding of both the Hebrew Bible's and John's Gospel portrays the indwelling of the Holy Spirit.[162]

Simeon Zahl uses the psychology of relational experience and social emotions as a lens to intervene in recent debates in Pauline soteriology.[163]

---

[158] Indeed, one way to read the Scientific Revolution is as an attempt by reformist Puritan natural philosophers (Boyle, Hooker, etc) to redirect the theological power of experience into a less revolutionary and more conservative form. Jacob and Jacob 1980, 251–67.

[159] Zahl 2020. For a response, see Leidenhag 2022b.

[160] Harrison 2016, 754. Kathryn Tanner also points out that the charismatic office of prophets or monks in the earliest centuries of the church were 'publicly evidenced and communally recognized. Their acquisition, moreover, is generally recognized to require slow and patient processes of training – for example, ascetic discipline'. Tanner 2010, 287.

[161] See Lauden 1977. [162] Kroll 2021. [163] Zahl 2021.

This brings us to the source of Scripture. When issues like Darwinian evolution and Genesis 1–2 dominate, as they too often do, then it seems inevitable that Scriptural authority will be pitted against scientific authority. If they are not in Conflict, the best we can hope for is a truce. Such a truce is sometimes captured in the divide between the Book of Scripture and the Book of Nature metaphor, and the division of theology into 'revealed theology' and 'natural theology'. But such categories conceal the constant interplay between the various methods of Scriptural interpretation and the methods of empirical investigation. It is impossible to disentangle the allegorical method of Scriptural interpretation and the delightful details of medieval bestiaries. Luther's prioritizing of the plain-text readings, and Huldrych Zwingli's more exclusive insistence on the 'natural sense of Scripture' should be part of any story of the intellectual origins of the scientific revolution.[164] The rise of historical-critical hermeneutics in the late nineteenth century was an attempt at a new scientific approach to Scripture, a correspondence that became explicit in Rudolf Bultmann's project of demythologization. This story has not ended and we continue to see how new scientific methods for reading nature are applied to biblical scholarship, as in cognitive linguistics, and as postmodern theories of reading impact scientific thought and practice. A science-engaged theology project may use social psychology to evaluate Pauline exegesis, as Simeon Zahl has done, or it might use cognitive linguistics to analyse the Gospels, as Elizabeth Shively suggests, or it might draw on contemporary botany to explore the biblical metaphor of grafting, as in Kimberly Kroll's work.[165]

The sciences can be used as a source in a myriad of ways. If we stick too closely to the Wesleyan quadrilateral then it might seem like, as part of experience, science can only vivify. What might it mean for a scientific theory to vivify doctrine? Hopefully it will not descend to what Jonathan Jong fears, 'the old preacher's trick of saying, after recounting some anodyne personal anecdote, "and doesn't that rather remind us of Jesus?". That which makes for bad preaching also makes for bad theology, science-engaged or otherwise'.[166] This makes for bad theology because it is a trick. Like shady ad men in the sixties, it makes you feel like you experienced something real (engaged science in a meaningful way), whereas in reality it was just a catchy slogan. If the sciences are part of what Wesley means by 'confirmed by reason' then we are left with little more than fact checking. This runs the risk of treating science naïvely as a kind of data mine, rather than as diverse practices of inquiry and traditions of interpretation.

The sciences do not exhaust, and so are not identical to, what is often meant by religious experience, reason, Scripture and church tradition. Sometimes it might

---

[164] See Fraser 2018.   [165] Kroll 2021; Shively and Rüggemeier 2021; Zahl 2021.
[166] Jong 2021, 484.

make sense to think of the sciences as a series of additional sources set apart from these traditional four, but much of the time it will not. What we end up with, then, is a reminder that the sources of theology are not natural kinds. There is a plurality of legitimate and helpful ways to count the sources of theology. Sometimes we need to say there is one source, the Holy Spirit, or God in God's self-revelation, or something like that. Sometimes we need to say there are three or four sources, in order to make our claims from one source open to critique and accountability from others. Sometimes we might want to, 'ask the beasts' (Job 12:7), and say there are hundreds of sources in order to show the glory of God who is beyond all creaturely knowing and speaks through the diversity of the created world.

5.3 How to Engage the Sciences as Sources for Theology?

5.3.1 Search for Risks

Should science-engaged theology be risky theology? If so, why? Not for the reasons stated in our discussion of Popper from Section 4.2; that is, science-engaged theology doesn't seek to demarcate real theology, which takes risks and engages with scientific studies, from pseudo-theology, which doesn't. Not all theology need be science-engaged and not all theology needs to 'stick its neck out' – or be risky, in our sense. However, sometimes it does, and sometimes theologians already make risky claims and need to be held to account.

Consider an example which doesn't employ science but will be familiar to any theologian: a claim about *what Paul said* (or Luther or Thomas or whoever). Delivering on such a claim takes sound exegesis, literacy in Greek or Latin, reading with appropriate historical sensitivity, and so on. We already see the place for prolonged discussions which hold people accountable for such claims. But theologians already routinely make empirical claims, perhaps more often than they realise. Whether it's about *what Paul said*, or a more obviously empirical claim like Calvin's *predestination provides consolation through the storms of life*, we can see the success criteria that needs to be met. And why is that good? Not because of some allegedly neutral principle of verification or falsification but because clear success criteria allow theologians to prune wrong or idolatrous ideas. The tools of the empirical sciences allow theologians to be risky, and thus serve the church, in exactly this way.

Another example, this one from real life: John Milbank has been one of the most innovative theologians of the past generation. His deconstruction of the reigning orthodoxy of the secular academy has influenced not only theology but social science as well. Being innovative, however, is not the same as taking risks. His obscurantic prose often defies disagreement *or* agreement. This makes Arne Rasmusson's article-length reply to Milbank's political theology especially worthwhile. We see it as demonstrating one way to pursue science-engaged theology.

Even though Rasmusson doesn't use the language of riskiness, it's clear that he has something like this in view. He focuses on *The Politics of Virtue* because it is here, perhaps more than any other of Milbank's titles, that Milbank and his co-author Adrian Pabst stick their necks out. That fact makes it *better theology*, not because riskiness is inherently good but, because the authors write in such a way that they can be held accountable. To take just one example:

> Milbank and Pabst claim that Catholicism has more potential to create the necessary social trust than the more pessimistic anthropological understandings of Protestantism and its various legacies. They construe this also as a historical and sociological claim. They could also very well have constructed this as a hypothesis that might be tested against historical and statistical data. It so happens that there are numerous studies that try to measure the correlation between religious cultures and the degree of social trust.[167]

And what do such studies show? Their findings are the exact opposite to those predicted by Milbank and Pabst; in fact, Protestant countries have more social trust.[168] Again, this capacity to be proved wrong is a *strength* of the book. What would make for an even stronger book, however, would be if Milbank and Pabst had engaged the scientific studies themselves, rather than left it to their readers. Rasmusson continues: 'these findings are well-known, but they are not something that Milbank and Pabst discuss ... If these claims are not supported, this ought to lead to some rethinking. Maybe other factors also play a role. But Milbank and Pabst do not even ask the question'.[169]

Another of Rasmusson's examples is Milbank's response to the Brexit referendum, the result of which was not to Milbank's liking: 'tragically, the Reformation, Roundhead, nonconformist, puritan, whig, capitalist, liberal version of Britishness last night triumphed over our deep ancient character which is Catholic or Anglican, Cavalier, Jacobite, High Tory or Socialist'. Except when Rasmusson investigated the numbers, it hardly supported that conclusion. 'If one uses Milbank's unqualified language, one might say that it seems to have been rather the nonconformist, puritan, whig, capitalist and liberal England that supported Remain ... In terms of religious affiliation it is precisely the Anglicans that stand out as a group overwhelmingly (60-40%) supporting Brexit in contrast to other Christian groups'.[170]

Thus, Milbank displays the virtue of empirical accountability – albeit ironically. Implicit in Rasmusson's argument, and explicit in ours, is the claim that

---

[167] Rasmusson 2021, 55.   [168] Rasmusson 2021, 53.   [169] Rasmusson 2021, 57.
[170] Rasmusson 2021, 58.

accountable theology is better theology. We should not be misunderstood as saying that empirical theology is always better. Theology's criteria of assent are *supposed* to differ according to the claim in question. We all know that when theologians make historical claims, they should use the best historical scholarship. Likewise, with biblical scholarship, and likewise with empirical claims and scientific studies. Rasmusson writes, 'Milbank and Pabst open themselves to such criticisms because of the laudable historical and social concreteness of their accounts and the many specific claims they make'.[171] Making concrete claims is good, but there follows an obligation to substantiate.

But does science-engaged theology mean that empirical tools are always proving theologians wrong? Does this not place the Gospel under constant threat? Such a defensive worry carries with it (again) the misguided picture of science and religion as discrete and potentially competing territories. But there is also an additional reason not to worry.

In 1953 W.V.O. Quine published one of the most widely read papers of the century, entitled, 'Two Dogmas of Empiricism'. One of Quine's rebuttals to the two dogmas was holism, the principle that a single hypothesis or prediction comes with a whole network of background assumptions, such that any theory is underdetermined by the data that supports it. What this means is that when one receives a negative result from an experiment, you never know for sure if the theory you are attempting to expose is at fault, or if it is some other auxiliary premise that is the culprit. A famous example comes from the attempt to test Newtonian dynamics by observation of planetary positions.[172] When Leverrier and Adams observed irregularities in the orbits of Uranus and Mercury, they were faced with a decision; declare Newtonian dynamics falsified or posit an unobserved additional planet. In the case of Uranus, they chose the latter, and with the discovery of Neptune were proved right. An explanation for Mercury's odd behaviour was not provided until Newtonian dynamics was replaced with relativistic mechanics.

Declaring a theory falsified in light of some observation or anomalous result ends up being, in Popper's words, 'a free decision' or a 'trial by jury', that practitioners make at various stages by weighing a diverse range of criteria, not all of which will be empirical or even rational.[173] An important consequence of this is that theologians are not compelled to give up on their favoured interpretation of a doctrine when one or two studies seem to contradict their predictions. In explaining how saintly relics work, Thomas Aquinas seems to suggest that the medicinal properties of rhubarb (rhubarb!) are caused by planetary motion.[174] Because he was wrong about rhubarb, what follows? Probably not

---

[171] Rasmusson 2021, 60.   [172] This example is taken from Dupré 1993, 231.
[173] Popper 2002, 92.   [174] Heßbrüggen-Walter 2014, 322–6; cf. Aquinas 1939.

much. Or does Melanchthon's mistaken idea that the human mind is made up of two distinct faculties, reason and affect, mean that we have to abandon his version of the doctrine of justification by faith alone, which is built upon this psychology?[175] This is a more difficult case, although the answer is still probably no. Theological ideas are complex beasts and the more longstanding or tradition-approved a doctrine is the wider range of criteria will likely impact one's assent and dissent; biblical warrant, pastoral impact and the knock-on effect on other doctrinal areas, to name a few. One, or even several, recent empirical studies are not sufficient to entirely take-out longstanding theological doctrines. Pruning theological ideas with empirical accountability cannot be done in haste. There is slow and patient work to be done in looking at each of these on a case-by-case basis.

5.3.2 Search for Entanglements

Even our friendliest critic could reasonably respond that if Rasmusson is our model, our vision of science-engaged theology appears limited to empirical fact checking. Fact checking is oftentimes an authentically theological task, but science-engaged theology is not *only* that. We also think theologians should pay careful attention to points of entanglement, where a claim requires the tools of more than one discipline to understand.

Entanglement is similar, in some respects, to how Gould deconstructed his own map metaphor: the so-called non-overlapping magisteria are often *inter-digitating*. This conveys that the supposed no man's land is really an *everyone's* land. Here we consider two different types of entanglement: (1) conjunctive entanglements, where the conjunction of two non-entangled concepts forms a newly entangled claim, and (2) concept entanglements, where the base concepts being used are entangled in multiple disciplinary conversations, even when they are (in any given moment) being used in a single discipline.

An example of a conjunctive entanglement can be taken from earlier in this Element. For Roman Catholics, gluten-free bread is invalid matter for the celebration of the Eucharist. We know of the protein called gluten using the tools of modern chemistry, so by itself gluten isn't entangled. We know the concept of sacramental validity from Canon Law, and especially the *Summa Theologica*, so that isn't really entangled either. But put the concepts together (by talking about the sacramental validity of gluten) and you get a claim caught in the middle of Gould's no man's land. It is not only *claims* that get entangled; certain concepts are themselves already entangled, like matter, person, miracle

---

[175] The example of Melanchthon on this point was made by Simeon Zahl in a 2022 conference paper.

or, in this example, bread. Is matter a thing that has volume and mass, or a thing that has a substance and accident – or is it in some strange way, both? Is person 'a substance of a rational nature', a 'subsistent relation' or 'a thinking intelligent being, that has reason and reflection, and can consider itself as itself' – or none of the above?

In order to explain concept entanglement we will compare two examples. Both examples concern ordination, first of Black men in the practice of the Church of Jesus Christ of Latter-day Saints (LDS), and second of intersex individuals in Roman Catholic practice. On the surface, these two examples may appear similar, but they are importantly different.

5.3.3 Race-Based Ordination

Some nineteenth-century sources regarded as canon among LDS teach that Black people were cursed with darker skin because of misdeeds in a prior existence and so cannot be ordained. When Mormon missionaries encountered success in Brazil, even starting construction on a temple in São Paulo in 1975, they faced a problem. Brazil is 85 per cent multiracial. In such a racially diverse society, who counted as Black? It turned out that race was more complicated than the nineteenth-century canon anticipated. Around that time, LDS authorities stopped teaching that skin colour was a curse. Instead, they taught that God banned Blacks from the Mormon priesthood for God's own hidden reasons and the church is bound by this choice. For a while, would-be ordinands were interviewed about their family history, with the promise to report if they later learned of any Black ancestors.[176] In a time before widespread DNA testing, that strategy was eventually overwhelmed by the racial complexity of Brazil.[177] The local mission president reported, 'the ultimate recourse would be to consider the case carefully and then, if there was no assurance that they had Black lineage, to present the case to the Lord with a request that he would inspire or prompt the conferral of the priesthood. We knew unless He inspired us we [would] inevitably make mistakes'.[178] On June 1, 1978, four months before the planned dedication of the São Paulo Temple, members of the church's governing body were praying in Utah and heard God say that the ban on Black priests was lifted.[179]

5.3.4 Sex-Based Ordination

Attention to gender and sex is important in much of Christian theology, especially those churches that limit ordination to males. In Roman Catholic practice,

---

[176] Harris and Bringhurst 2015, 136–7.   [177] Harris and Bringhurst 2015, 112.
[178] Harris and Bringhurst 2015, 102.
[179] This story is simplified. For a fuller discussion, see Harris and Bringhurst 2015.

an invalidly ordained priest, such as a priest who is not male, was never in fact a priest and all the sacraments that person administered never happened. Historically, the reasons given for limiting the priesthood to men are to portray man's natural superiority over women, to make the symbolism of the Mass easy to recognize and to better portray the spousal love of a bridegroom (Jesus) for the bride (the Church).[180] The Catholic Catechism, which was commissioned by John Paul II in 1985, doesn't cite any of these reasons, only saying that it was Jesus' choice and 'the Church recognizes herself to be bound by this choice'.[181]

The markers of maleness are sometimes ambiguous among humans, in fact, for mammals in general. For example, mammals with Persistent Mullerian duct syndrome (PMDS) have both testes and ovaries. Can a human with PMDS be ordained as a Catholic priest? Well, it depends on what Canon Law means by male (Latin, *vir*). Does Canon Law mean 'person who identifies as male', which is what much of today's psychological sciences would mean, including some neuroscience? Or does Canon Law take its cue from the biological sciences? Like science and religion, terms like 'male' and 'female' are also not fixed transhistorical categories. The only evidence that biologists have access to are the empirical markers currently held to be indicative of this term:

- hormone ratios,
- chromosomes,
- gonads (the presence or absence of ovaries and testes),
- genitalia (the presence or absence of a clitoris and a penis) and
- secondary characteristics (among humans, vocal register and breast/hip shape).

If those markers are ambiguous or, as in the PMDS case, point in different directions, the biologist's reply is, 'from the evidence I have, I cannot determine if this individual is male or female; they are intersex'.

According to Catholic theology (or more precisely, according to some Thomist schools of thought that the Vatican regards as authoritative), *there are no intersex humans*. There are only humans that the tools of today's biology sometimes fail to classify. Every single human is, by definition, either male or female. Note that the biologist's statement, understood one way is compatible with this Thomist notion (the biologist is saying, 'I need more data') and, understood another way, poses tensions (such as if the biologist is saying, 'absent more data, the individual is neither male or female' – or alternatively, is both male and female).

---

[180] Respectively, these are the reasons associated with Aquinas, Paul VI, and John Paul II. See Inter Insigniores 1976; Aquinas 1981, Supp q.39 a1; Mulieris Dignitatem 1988.

[181] Catechism of the Catholic Church 1993, 1577.

5.3.5 Explaining Entanglement

So, are 'Black' and 'male' entangled concepts? When LDS authorities devised their doctrine of ordination, they were using race in a non-entangled way (or, *thought* they were; more on this point shortly). That is, they believed that whatever biologists or anthropologists meant by 'Black' was adequate as the criterion for purposes of the doctrine. Since it only took the tools of one discipline (to their minds) race was not entangled.[182] By contrast, the way that Catholic canon law understands maleness is entangled. Allow us to explain.

What tools do we need to understand what a male is? Well, *empirical* tools, starting with basic observation.[183] Sometimes even the most careful observer will need to know more, and then, observation with a microscope and blood tests could help, preferably with the ability to detect certain genes and hormone levels. The tools that biologists have access to now are different from those that they had at their disposal in previous centuries and, doubtless will be different in the future. But as things look now, even the most advanced biological tools would sometimes lead to the result, 'I don't know'.

At first glance, this sounds like what happened to the Mormon missionaries. Their doctrine specified, no Black priests. But in Brazil, they found themselves saying over and over, 'I don't know' if a certain man is Black. One missionary to Brazil recounted, 'I learned that it's impossible to tell by observation, or even by trying to establish facts, who had or had not [a Black] lineage'.[184] The empirical tools, namely observation, were not adequate. It was the phenomenon of interracial peoples that overwhelmed the doctrine, or was poised to, when the church was saved by *Deus ex machina* in June 1978. More sophisticated tools did eventually emerge – such as DNA ancestry tests, which ironically demonstrated that every human on Earth counts as Black by the Mormon rule – but be that as it may, whatever biology 'said' using biology's tools settled the matter of who was eligible for the priesthood. The sources of Mormon theology didn't say anything about who was Black, only that if they were, they couldn't be a priest.[185] This story of course is made far more complicated when one realizes that the whole concept of

---

[182] Although racial concepts are probably always entangled, we can say that the LDS church thought of 'Black' as not entangled on its own, just as the Vatican considers gluten in a non-entangled way. However, just as 'gluten cannot be consecrated' is entangled as a conjunctive statement, so would the prior LDS teaching, 'Blacks can't be ordained'.

[183] Let us emphasize here that we are not trying to police who is a man or a woman. If anything, the desire that many transpeople articulate to have one's body, pronouns, and sense of identity align shows the importance of using a wide range of tools, including those that study embodiment.

[184] Harris and Bringhurst 2015, 102.

[185] In fact, some later Mormon thinkers (but not the LDS church) suggested that 'Black' wasn't anything to do with skin colour; it was about having a sinful soul. *That* interpretation would have been entangled. See Mason 2018.

race has theological roots and meaning, which if incorporated into the LDS reasoning on ordination would have made it more consciously entangled.[186] But note, since an entangled concept is one that requires more than one discipline to understand it, what counts as entangled is not so much dependent upon the conscious awareness of the users of a concept, in this case the LDS leadership, as on the fragmentation or conjoining of disciplines.

This is *not* how Catholics or, at least, Vatican authorities, think of maleness. Again, making a very long story short, what biology says about maleness using the tools of their discipline is *entangled* with what theology says about maleness using theological tools such as philosophical reflection, the study of history including trusted authorities, biblical hermeneutics and the experience and witness of the faithful. Using those tools, Catholic theology defines maleness (and femaleness) somewhat differently than most of today's biologists.

For instance, here we cite an article by two theologians published by the Catholic Health Association. They clearly outline the presuppositions required before a Catholic account of sex can be offered.

> As 'a sure norm', the *Catechism* outlines four basic components of an authentically Christian anthropology: Human beings occupy 'a unique place in creation' as 1) created 'in the image of God'; 2) in our nature uniting 'the spiritual and material worlds'; 3) created 'male and female'; and 4) established by God in 'friendship'. ....
> The church's magisterium and moral tradition have generally affirmed the Thomistic thesis that human beings are essentially 'rational animals' comprising a material body informed by a rational soul [a tenet of Thomistic hylomorphism]. While strictly speaking the soul, which is immaterial, is not sexed ... as the vivifying principle of actually existing human beings, the human soul is properly characterized as sexed.[187]

So, given these presuppositions, how do they understand a person's sex? First, they rely on the usual biological markers, but they also add a constraint that rules out a minority of cases. Using biblical exegesis, they have concluded that 'God created them male and female' applies to each and every human without exception. A full understanding of sex, for these Roman Catholics, therefore includes both biological and biblical research.

It is a sign of science-engaged theology done well that neither field's sources automatically get to override the other. If we are serious about using tools of

---

[186] For more on race as a theological, or what we call entangled, concept see Kidd 2006; Carter 2008; Jennings 2010.
[187] Bedford and Eberl 2016, 20–1. For readability, we have removed internal citations from this quote.

multiple disciplines, there will be no universal decision procedure to say whose tools or sources count for more. Science-engaged theology seeks to promote careful attention to entangled concepts and claims, not necessarily resolve them. Science-engaged theology is not about disentangling, which would result in a new project of reductionism. This is one of the reasons we said that doing science-engaged theology well depends on narrow research topics, with explicit attention to the relevant *sub*-disciplines, be they scientific or theological. We want to keep the focus on the tools that are used to conceive of concepts in one or another way. We cannot decide a priori whether one set of tools will get us closer to the truth of the matter, or if we will continue to need both sets. This is also why we started the section by speaking of the porous nature of university faculties. Entanglement is not something to be avoided. Why? Theologians need help, handmaidens, to do their job.

Read more of John Perry's work on whether intersex persons could be ordained as Roman Catholic priests, including this reply from a Catholic philosopher.[188]

What science-engaged theology will resist, however, is anything that veers toward what we earlier called NOMA on steroids. Sticking with our example, if the Vatican suddenly released a statement declaring, 'Hold on, we only meant that "Vatican maleness™" is required for ordination; what biologists find is irrelevant', that would prevent biology from 'touching' theology, as if there was a bright border between the two.[189]

5.4 Conclusion

In this section we've given a more positive account of why theologians should want to engage the sciences, how the sciences relate to other sources for theological reflection, and suggested two ways that they might engage. We argued that the sciences aid theologians in hearing God's voice in the world by training them in virtues like empirical accountability. When we consider how the sciences fit alongside other theological sources our argument was

---

[188] Perry 2021; Rehman 2022.

[189] There is an example of this, applied to our case study, in an article aptly titled, 'Why Aquinas's Metaphysics of Gender Is Fundamentally Correct'. The relevant passage is deep in the weeds of an argument between two Thomists, who only disagree about who thinks that Aquinas was *more* right. We will spare you the details, but essentially one thinker proposes that the XX (or XY) chromosomes are 'little more than a sign to the Creator' to infuse a soul with feminine (or masculine) attributes, and whatever happens to chromosomes after God has infuse such a soul, doesn't matter in terms of sex or gender. Notice how the notion allows this Thomist to insist that every human is male or female without any possible negation. The chromosomes are a *private* sign, and crucially a *non-empirical* sign, which accomplish just what the more obvious NOMA on steroids did. Newton 2020, 202.

deconstructive. It is not helpful to count the sources or identify science with only one of the traditional four; such games only return to the errors of modernity explored in previous sections. Saying that the sciences should be engaged as sources of theological reflection does not yet tell us *how* to do so. We do not want to be too prescriptive here. There may be many more ways of engaging the sciences beyond our two ideas, but we emphasized entanglement and theology-as-risky as starting points.[190]

6 Conclusion: Advice to Those Who Would Be Science-Engaged Theologians

Science-engaged theology, as theology, is a form of faith seeking understanding. Therefore, it will typically not start with a scientific insight and draw a theological conclusion. Instead, science-engaged theology starts with theological questions on which empirical studies may shed some light. Here are more examples: Preston Hill re-examines Calvin's theology of Christ's descent into hell using the psychology of trauma.[191] Alexander Massmann extends recent theologies of grace, such as in John Barclay's work, through engagement with biological and zoological discoveries on non-human reciprocity.[192] Matthew Kuan Johnson and Rachel Siow Robertson use positive psychology, embodied cognition and ritual studies to answer the question, how can joy be a divine command if it is not within our control?[193]

What is common between all these studies is the level of specificity, both in terms of the theological question asked and the scientific insight drawn upon; the more granular and specific the better. The question is never '*can* x doctrine and y scientific theory *possibly* relate?' Nor do the best examples of science-engaged theology merely ask, '*how* do x doctrine and y scientific theory relate?' Instead, better questions are of the form: how does y finding shed new light, or correct a distortion, or corroborate a position in x theology. Just as a theology-engaged science could ask, how does theological discussion of x shed new light on, correct a distortion of, or corroborate the discussion of y in the sciences? Examples of this might be Andrew Davison's discussion of analogy in describing machine learning and artificial intelligence, which is informed by discussion of analogy in Thomas Aquinas, Thomas Cajetan and Francisco Suárez.[194] Another might be Joanna Leidenhag's analysis of the role of dialectic personalism in the origin of autism as a diagnostic category.[195] A third might be to

---

[190] Beyond the two we have suggested in this section, we can point to the three ways N. T. Wright proposes theologians use history: 'defeating the defeaters', 'dismantling the distortions', and 'directing the discussion'. Wright 2019, 121.
[191] Hill 2021.   [192] Massmann 2021.   [193] Johnson and Robertson 2022.
[194] Davison 2021, 254–74.   [195] Leidenhag 2020, 125.

interrogate often individualistic and subjective definitions of flourishing in much positive psychology and social science.

Returning to science-engaged theology, some of these theological questions might be practical in nature. Does believing that God can suffer improve or reduce psychological wellbeing? Should Christians eat plant-based food? Do Christians who say the creed in different languages profess the same faith? To answer any of these questions, at the very least, theologians need accurate and nuanced understanding of the physical and psychological situations at hand. But science-engaged theology is not always so immediately practical; there are many types of theology that speak of created realities. This includes human cognitive processes (such as faith, belief, or hope), spiritual practices, or character formation, claims about sin, claims about other creatures, claims about church polity, liturgy, or sacraments, claims about the incarnation, about birth and death. All these claims are *theological claims about empirical realities*, and so theologians should partner with those trained in various empirical methods of investigation. That is the basic principle of science-engaged theology. Whenever theologians, of whatever kind, make claims about created, empirical realities, they should incorporate the insights of empirical investigation into their analysis. Science-engaged theology is not a way for 'science' and 'religion' to relate, like placing two bodies of knowledge in dialogue or integrating two types of intellectual practice. We prefer to think of science-engaged theology as a disposition or mindset.

In his influential paper, 'The Plurality of Science', Patrick Suppes tells a story about how his daughter, who was working towards her PhD, gave him a subscription to the (supposedly expository) journal, *Neurosciences: Research Program Bulletin*. Like a good father, Suppes tried to learn about his daughter's passion, but he found the articles utterly unintelligible. Suppes comments, 'the experimental literature is simply impossible to penetrate without a major learning effort'.[196] One doesn't have to know everything in a scientific field in order to engage with it, but one does need to be able to read articles of specific studies and be able to speak enough 'science-ese' to create a pidgin language (just as the scientist might need some 'Christian-ese' to work with Christian theologians). Even these pidgin languages can take substantial effort. While more popular science books would make this work easier, such texts are often unifiers: creating grand theories, and speculating about further connections and implications that are not warranted by the underlying studies.[197] If nothing else has convinced you yet, then the difficulty of learning a new language is a pragmatic reason to limit yourself to engaging with science in a highly localized way.

---

[196] Suppes 1993, 45.   [197] Barrett 2022.

6.1 Rules of Thumb

Descriptions are always implicitly normative. The principle with which we began, *memento naturam*, is simple enough, but doing science-engaged theology well can be a difficult task. As such, here we have collected some of the practical take-home messages from the preceding sections.

Section 2: Beyond the Territories of Science and Religion

- Avoid using 'science' and 'religion' as if these were transhistorical or trans-geographical categories.
- Recognize that thinkers in different (historical or geographical) cultures to your own may have a different understanding of what counts as a scientific or a theological claim, and a different idea of what gives such claims legitimacy.
- Consider the impact that mid-level historical patterns may be having on the scientific theory, methodology or sub-discipline that you are seeking to engage. Recognize that these patterns and their impact are contingent social factors.
- Be aware of the local, political and sociological issues surrounding particular studies and interpretations of data.
- Be suspicious if your localized science-engaged theology project or analysis fits too neatly and tidily into mythological categories or metanarratives.

Section 3: Neither Serf Nor Queen: Theology's New Boldness in the University

- Do not attempt to use the sciences uncritically as a way to prove theology's academic credentials in the university.
- Do not be embarrassed or coy about the particularity of theology's truth claims.
- Science-engaged theology need not be a version of natural theology but should deal with the revelation of God in its historical and ecclesial particularity.
- Try not to lose sight of how Christian concepts and claims operate within a wider theological narrative even as you take such narrative-laden claims into a new linguistic context (just as we say for the scientific claims and pidgin languages in Section 4).
- Do not hesitate to use the sciences to further the aims and goals of theology, even when these aims are in tension with those of the scientific project you are engaging.
- Furthering the aims and goals of theology means that most science-engaged theology projects will start with a question or problem that arises out of a particular theological project.

- Do not suppose that theology has all the answers or can dictate the appropriate methods, frameworks, goals and content of other disciplines. To think of theology as the queen of the sciences in this way would only be to refuse to learn from what the Spirit might be doing in those other disciplines.
- Recognize theology's need for helpers. Be confident enough in theology to recognize your own (and your theological hero's) indebtedness to the patient endeavours of those outside of your own discipline.

Section 4: Unity and Pluralism in Science

- Be as specific as you can. Do your best to see if these claims can be corroborated with current knowledge in the relevant disciplines of enquiry that specialize in this topic.
- Find the concepts that scientists are currently using that seem to best match the ideas you seek to test. Remember that words change their meaning across intellectual traditions.
- Work hard at developing a trading zone and accept that your communication may be a pidgin language.
- Talking to people who speak a different 'native language' to your own, who can explain the different resonances of terms, will often allow you to develop a more useful pidgin than solely reading scientific work.
- This is not a project of translation or reduction. Make sure to return to your native tongue with your hard-earned learning. Don't let your pidgin turn in to creole.
- Seek to understand the assumptions, aims and methods of the scientific field you are engaging. Bear these in mind when you are assessing the import of a particular finding for your own work.
- Rely on peer-review articles and literature reviews on particular topics, rather than popular level science books that unify and universalize particular findings.

Section 5: The Sciences among the Sources of Theology

- Make risky claims in your theology that might be tested in some way.
- Do not overuse your secateurs. You do not always need to abandon your theological idea or model simply because a few studies looking at analogous ideas seem to falsify it.
- Remember that data are theory-laden and theories are part of a wider web of meaning. These studies may motivate you to abandon your theological idea, but they do not mandate it.
- Recognize when your work is making claims that would benefit from the tools of other disciplines.

- Value epistemic virtues such as empirical accountability, coherence with other things we know (in theology and beyond) and be willing to expose your work to criticism from the widest variety of sources.
- Search for entangled claims or concepts, which require more than one discipline to understand.
- Although the balance between disciplinary perspectives in understanding entangled concepts may not always be equal, you should resist the temptation to resolve entangled concepts in any single disciplinary direction.
- Remember that the sciences are implicated in, but do not exhaust, the other standard sources of theological reflection: scripture, tradition, reason and experience.
- Do not associate 'science' with just one source or use it as a trump card over against other theological traditions.
- Do not be shy about changing your mind.

Appendix: Examples Cited

Arnold, Paul (2022). What Are the Theological Implications of Understanding Gestures as a Fundamental Part of Language and Thought? Theological Puzzles (6). www.theo-puzzles.ac.uk/2022/03/17/parnold.

Cockayne, Joshua and Gideon Salter (2021). Feasts of Memory: Collective Remembering, Liturgical Time Travel and the Actualisation of the Past. Modern Theology. doi.org/10.1111/moth.12683.

Hill, Preston (2021). Does God Need a Body to Keep the Score of Trauma? Theological Puzzles (1). www.theo-puzzles.ac.uk/2021/04/20/phill.

Johnson, Matthew Kuan and Rachel Siow Robertson (2022). How Can Joy be a Divine Command if it is not Within Our Control? Theological Puzzles (7). www.theo-puzzles.ac.uk/2022/05/02/robertson-johnson.

Kroll, Kimberly (2021). How Might Grafting Elucidate Our Understanding of the Indwelling Relation of the Holy Spirit and the Human Person? Theological Puzzles (4). www.theo-puzzles.ac.uk/2021/11/02/kkroll.

Leidenhag, Joanna (2022a). Does Embryology Elucidate a Traducianist View of the Origin of the Soul? Theological Puzzles (6). www.theo-puzzles.ac.uk/2022/03/17/jleidenhag2.

Lougheed, Kirk (2021). Are There Empirically Informed Solutions to the Problem of Religious Disagreement? Theological Puzzles (3). www.theo-puzzles.ac.uk/2021/09/06/klougheed.

Massmann, Alexander (2021). Should We Understand Grace in Altruistic or Reciprocal Terms? Theological Puzzles (1). www.theo-puzzles.ac.uk/2021/04/20/amassmann.

Pedersen, Daniel J. (2021). Is It Just for God to Damn for Sins Which Have Evolutionary Causes? Theological Puzzles (1). www.theo-puzzles.ac.uk/2021/03/26/dpedersen.

Perry, John (2021). Can Intersex Persons be Ordained as Catholic Priests Theological Puzzles (2). www.theo-puzzles.ac.uk/2021/06/05/jperry.

Rehman, Rashad (2022). What is Intersex? A Reply to Perry's Applied Moral Theology of Sex, Intersex and Ordination, Theological Puzzles (7). www.theo-puzzles.ac.uk/2022/05/02/rehman.

Scrutton, Tasia (2021). Can a Period of Mental Distress be Both a Dark Night of the Soul and a Mental Illness at the Same Time? Theological Puzzles (2). www.theo-puzzles.ac.uk/2021/06/05/tscrutton.

Sollereder, Bethany (2021). Can Theology Help Us Understand the Human Role in Environmental Restoration? Theological Puzzles (3). www.theo-puzzles.ac.uk/2021/08/28/bsollereder.

Tausen, Brittany and Katherine Douglass (2021). Can the Tools of Social-Cognitive Psychology Inform Spiritual Formation Practices? Theological Puzzles (4). www.theo-puzzles.ac.uk/2021/10/21/tausen-douglass.

Zahl, Simeon (2021). Beyond the Critique of Soteriological Individualism: Relationality and Social Cognition. Modern Theology. doi.org/10.1111/moth.12686.

References

Aquinas, Thomas (1929). *Scriptum super Libros sententiarum Magistri Petri Lombardi*. R. P. Mandonnet, ed. Paris: Lethielleux.

Aquinas, Thomas (1939). *A Letter of Thomas Aquinas to a Certain Knight Beyond the Mountainson the Occult Workings of Nature of Heavenly Bodies*. Translated Joseph Bernard McAllister. Washington D.C.: Catholic University of America Press. 70–80.

Aquinas, Thomas (1981). *Summa Theologiae*. Fathers of the English Dominican Province, trans. Notre Dame, IN: Ave Marie Press.

Arnold, Paul (2022). What Are the Theological Implications of Understanding Gestures as a Fundamental Part of Language and Thought? *Theological Puzzles* (6). www.theo-puzzles.ac.uk/2022/03/17/parnold/.

Barbour, Ian (1966). *Issues in Science and Religion*. Englewood, NJ: Prentice Hall.

Barbour, Ian (1974). *Myths, Models and Paradigms: A Comparative Study in Science and Religion*. New York: HarperCollins.

Barrett, Justin L (2022). *TheoPsych: A Psychological Science Primer for Theologians*. Knoxville, TN: Blueprint 1543.

Barth, Karl (1934). *Nein! Antwort an Emil Brunner*. Munich: C. Kaiser.

Barth, Karl (1961). *Church Dogmatics*, 4 vols. Peabody, MA: Hendrickson.

Bedford, Elliott Louis and Eberl, Jason T. (2016). Is the Soul Sexed? Anthropology, Transgenderism, and Disorders of Sex Development. *Healthcare Ethics USA*, 24(3), 18–33.

Bonaventura (2013). *De Reductione Artium ad Theologiam*. Emma Therese Healy, trans. and ed. Whitefish, MT: Literary Licensing LLC.

Breward, Ian (1974). Hooker, Richard. J.D. Douglas, eds., *The New International Dictionary of the Christian Church*. Exeter: The Paternoster Press.

Brightman, Edgar S. (1937). An Empirical Approach to God. *Philosophical Review* 46, 147–69.

Brooke, John Hedley and Cantor, Geoffrey (1998). *Reconstructing Nature: The Engagement of Science and Religion*. Oxford: Oxford University Press.

Cantor, Geoffrey and Kenny, Chris (2001). Barbour's Fourfold Way: Problems with His Taxonomy of Science-Religion Relationships. *Zygon: Journal of Religion and Science,* 36(4), 765–81.

Carter, J. Cameron (2008). *Race: A Theological Account*. Oxford: Oxford University Press.

Cartwright, Nancy (1999). *The Dappled World: A Study of the Boundaries of Science*. Cambridge: Cambridge University Press.

Cat, Jordi, Cartwright, Nancy and Chang, Hasok (1996). Otto Neurath: Politics and the Unity of Science. Peter Galison and David J. Stump, eds., *Disunity and Contextualism*. Stanford, CA: Stanford University Press, 347–52.

Catechism of the Catholic Church (1993). Vatican. www.vatican.va/archive/ccc/index.htm.

Cavanaugh, William T. (1995). 'A Fire Strong Enough to Consume the House': The Wars of Religion and the Rise of the Nation State. *Modern Theology*, 11(4), 397–420.

Cavanaugh, William T. (2009). *The Myth of Religious Violence: Secular Ideology and the Roots of Modern Conflict*. Oxford: Oxford University Press.

Clayton, Philip (1998). *God and Contemporary Science*. Grand Rapids, MI: Eerdmans.

Clement of Alexandria (1991). *The Stromata, or Miscellanies*. New York: Catholic Press of America.

Creath, Richard (2021). Logical Empiricism. Edward N. Zalta, ed., *The Stanford Encyclopedia of Philosophy*. https://plato.stanford.edu/archives/win2021/entries/logical-empiricism.

D'Costa, Gavin (2011). On Theology, the Humanities, and the University. Christopher Craig Brittain and Francesca Aran Murphy, eds., *Theology, University, Humanities: Initium Sapientiae Timor Domini*. Eugene, OR: Cascade, 194–212.

Davison, Andrew (2021). Machine Learning and Theological Traditions of Analogy. *Modern Theology*, 37(2), 254–74.

Dewey, John (1938). Unity of Science as a Social Problem. Otto Neurath, Rudolf Carnap, and Charles Morris, eds., *The International Encyclopedia of Unified Science*. Chicago, IL: University of Chicago Press, 29–38.

Draper, John William (1875). *History of the Conflict between Religion and Science*. New York: Appleton.

Drees, William B. (1996). *Religion, Science, and Naturalism*. Cambridge: Cambridge University Press.

Dupré, John (1993). *The Disorder of Things: Metaphysical Foundations of the Disunity of Science*. Cambridge, MA: Cambridge University Press.

Dupré, Louis (2008). *The Enlightenment and the Intellectual Foundations of Modern Culture*. London, U.K.: Yale University Press.

Feyerabend, Paul (1993). *Against Method*. 3rd ed. London: Verso.

Fraser, Liam (2018). *Atheism, Fundamentalism, and the Protestant Reformation: Uncovering the Secret Sympathy*. Cambridge: Cambridge University Press.

Galilei, Galileo (1957). Letter from Galileo to Madama Christina, the Grand Duchess Dowager. Stillman Drake, ed., *Discoveries and Opinions of Galileo*. New York: Anchor-Doubleday, 173–216.

Galison, Peter (1996a). Introduction: The Context of Disunity. Peter Galison and David J. Stump, eds., *The Disunity of Science: Boundaries, Contexts, and Power*. Stanford, CA: Stanford University Press, 1–36.

Galison, Peter (1996b). Computer Simulations and the Trading Zone. Peter Galison and David J. Stump, eds., *The Disunity of Science: Boundaries, Contexts, and Power*. Stanford, CA: Stanford University Press, 118–57.

Galison, Peter (2016). Meanings of Scientific Unity: The Law, the Orchestra, the Pyramid, the Quilt and the Ring. Harmke Kamminga and Geert Somsen, eds., *Pursing the Unity of Science: Ideology and Scientific Practice from the Great War to the Cold War*. Abingdon: Routledge, 12–29.

Giere, Ronald (2006). Perspectival Pluralism. Longion Kellert, Helen Longino and C. Kenneth Waters, eds., *Scientific Pluralism*. Minneapolis, MN: University of Minnesota Press, 26–41.

Giles, J. (1863). Our Colonization and Its Ethics. *Southern Monthly Magazine*, 1(March), 549.

Godfrey-Smith, Peter (2003). *Theory and Reality: An Introduction to the Philosophy of Science*. Chicago, IL: University of Chicago Press.

Gould, Stephen Jay (1995). *Dinosaur in a Haystack: Reflections in Natural History*. Cambridge, MA: Harvard University Press.

Gould, Stephen Jay (1997). Non-overlapping Magisteria. *Natural History*, 106, 16–22.

Gould, Stephen Jay (2002). *Rocks of Ages: Science and Religion in the Fullness of Life*. London: Random House.

Gould, Stephen Jay (2011). *Leonardo's Mountain of Clams and the Diet of Worms: Essays in Natural History*. Reprint. Cambridge, MA: Harvard University Press.

Grey, Carmody (2021). A Theologian's Perspective on Science-Engaged Theology. *Modern Theology*, 37(2), 489–94.

Gustafson, James (2013). The Sectarian Temptation: Reflections on Theology, the Church and the University. *Proceedings of the Catholic Theological Society of America*, 40, 83–94.

Harris, Matthew L. and Bringhurst, Newell G. (2015). *The Mormon Church and Blacks: A Documentary History*. Chicago, IL: University of Illinois.

Harrison, Peter (2015). *The Territories of Science and Religion*. Chicago, IL: University of Chicago Press.

Harrison, Peter (2016). The Modern Invention of 'Science and Religion': What Follows. *Zygon: Journal of Religion and Science*, 53(1), 742–57.

Harrison, Peter (2019). Conflict, Complexity, and Secularization in the History of Science and Religion. Bernard Lightman, ed., *Rethinking History, Science, and Religion*. Pittsburgh, PA: University of Pittsburgh Press, 221–34.

Hauerwas, Stanley (1999). *After Christendom? How to Behave if Freedom, Justice, and a Christian Nation are Bad Ideas*. Nashville, TN: Abingdon Press.

Hauerwas, Stanley (2001). Why the 'Sectarian Temptation' is a Misrepresentation: A Response to James Gustafson. John Berkman and Michael Cartwright, eds., *The Hauerwas Reader*. London: Duke University Press, 90–4.

Hauerwas, Stanley (2007). *The State of the University: Academic Knowledges and the Knowledge of God*. Malden, MA: Blackwell.

Hauerwas, Stanley (2015). How to Think Theologically About Rights. *Journal of Law and Religion*, 30(October), 402–13.

Haught, John (1995). *Science & Religion: From Conflict to Conversion*. New York: Paulist Press.

Heßbrüggen-Walter, Stefan (2014). Problems with Rhubarb: Accommodating Experience in Aristotelian Theories of Science. *Early Science and Medicine*, 19, 317–40.

Hesse, Mary B. (1961a). *Forces and Fields: The Concept of Action at a Distance in the History of Physics*. Mineola, NY: Dover.

Hesse, Mary B. (1961b). *Science and the Human Imagination: Aspects of the History of Logic of Physical Science*. London: SCM Press.

Hesse, Mary B. (1980). *Revolutions and Reconstructions in the Philosophy of Science*. Bridgton: Indiana University Press.

Hesse, Mary B. and Arbib, Michael (1987). *The Construction of Reality*. Cambridge: Cambridge University Press.

Hill, Preston (2021). Does God Need a Body to Keep the Score of Trauma? *Theological Puzzles* (1). www.theo-puzzles.ac.uk/2021/04/20/phill.

Hodge, Charles (1871). *Systematic Theology*, 3 vols. New York: Scribner's Sons.

Holm, John (2012). *An Introduction to Pidgins and Creoles*. Cambridge: Cambridge University Press.

Inter Insigniores (1976). Vatican: Sacred Congregation for the Doctrine of the Faith. www.vatican.va/roman_curia/congregations/cfaith/documents/rc_con_cfaith_doc_19761015_inter-insigniores_en.html.

Jacob, James R. and Jacob, Margaret C. (1980). The Anglican Origins of Modern Science: The Metaphysics Foundations of the Whig Constitution. *Isis*, 71(2), 251–67.

Jardine, Nicholas (2018). Mary Brenda Hesse. *Biographical Memoirs of Fellows of the British Academy*, 17, 19–28.

Jefferson, Thomas (1826). Letter from Thomas Jefferson to Roger C. Weightman. *Declaring Independence: Drafting the Documents*. www .loc.gov/exhibits/declara/rcwltr.html.

Jennings, Willie J. (2010). *The Christian Imagination*. London: Yale University Press.

Johnson, Matthew Kuan and Robertson, Rachel Siow (2022). How Can Joy be a Divine Command if it is not Within Our Control? *Theological Puzzles* (7). www.theo-puzzles.ac.uk/2022/05/02/robertson-johnson.

Jong, Jonathan (2021). A Scientist's Perspective on Science-Engaged Theology. *Modern Theology*, 37(2), 483–88.

Kellert, Longion, Longino, Helen and Waters, C. Kenneth, eds. (2006). Introduction. *Scientific Pluralism*. Minneapolis, MN: University of Minnesota Press, vii–xxix.

Kidd, Colin (2006). *The Forging of the Races: Race and Scripture in the Protestant Atlantic World*. Cambridge: Cambridge University Press.

Kroll, Kimberly (2021). How Might Grafting Elucidate Our Understanding of the Indwelling Relation of the Holy Spirit and the Human Person? *Theological Puzzles* (4). www.theo-puzzles.ac.uk/2021/11/02/kkroll/.

Kuhn, Thomas S. (1970). *The Structure of Scientific Revolutions*. Chicago, IL: University of Chicago Press.

Lauden, Larry (1977). *Progress and Its Problems: Towards a Theory of Scientific Growth*. Rerkeley and Los Angeles, California: University of California Press.

Leclerc, Jean, ed. (1703–6). *Desiderii Erasmi Roterodami Opera Omnia*, 2 vols. Leiden: Brill.

Leidenhag, Joanna (2020). The Challenge of Autism for Relational Approach to Theological Anthropology. *International Journal of Systematic Theology*, 23 (1), 109–34.

Leidenhag, Joanna (2022a). Does Embryology Elucidate a Traducianist View of the Origin of the Soul? *Theological Puzzles* (6). www.theo-puzzles.ac.uk/ 2022/03/17/jleidenhag2/.

Leidenhag, Joanna (2022b). Response #2. *Journal of Soul Care and Spiritual Formation*, 15(1), 143–52.

Lightman, Bernard (2019). *Rethinking History, Science, and Religion: An Exploration of Conflict and the Complexity Principle*. Pittsburg, PA: University of Pittsburg Press.

Lindbeck, George (1984). *The Nature of Doctrine: Religion and Theology in a Postliberal Age*. Louisville, KY: Westminster John Knox Press.

Lindbeck, George (1989). Response to Bruce Marshall. *The Thomist: A Speculative Quarterly Review*, 53(3), 403–6.

Lindberg, David and Numbers, Ronald (1986). Beyond War and Peace: A Reappraisal of the Encounter between Christianity and Science. *Perspectives on Science and Christian Faith*, 39(3), 140–9.

Livingstone, David (2003). *Putting Science in its Place: Geographies of Scientific Knowledge.* Chicago, IL: University of Chicago Press.

Livingstone, David (2014). *Dealing with Darwin: Place, Politics, and Rhetoric in Religious Engagements with Evolution.* Baltimore, MD: Johns Hopkins University Press.

Locke, John (1975). *An Essay Concerning Human Understanding.* Peter H. Nidditch, ed. Oxford: Clarendon Press.

Lougheed, Kirk (2021). Are There Empirically Informed Solutions to the Problem of Religious Disagreement? *Theological Puzzles* (3). www.theo-puzzles.ac.uk/2021/09/06/klougheed/.

Mahmood, Saba (2012). *The Politics of Piety: The Islamic Revival and the Feminist Subject.* Princeton, NJ: Princeton University Press.

Martinson, Mattias (2013). Postliberal Theology. Anna L.C. Runehov and Lluis Oviedo, eds., *Encyclopedia of Sciences and Religion.* Dordrecht: Springer, 1817–23.

Mason, Patrick Q. (2018). Mormonism and Race. Paul Harvey and Kathryn Gin Lum, eds., *The Oxford Handbook of Religion and Race in American History.* Oxford: Oxford University Press, 156–71.

Massmann, Alexander (2021). Should We Understand Grace in Altruistic or Reciprocal Terms? *Theological Puzzles* (1). www.theo-puzzles.ac.uk/2021/04/20/amassmann.

McCormack, Bruce L. (2008). *Orthodox and Modern: Studies in the Theology of Karl Barth.* Grand Rapids, MI: Baker Academic.

McCutcheon, Russell T. (1997). 'My Theory of the Brontosaurus': Postmodernism and 'Theory' of Religion. *Studies in Religion/Sciences Religieuses*, 26(1), 3–23.

McCutcheon, Russell T. (2005). Introduction. Russell T. McCutcheon, ed., *The Insider/Outsider Problem: A Reader.* London: Continuum, 15–22.

McCutcheon, Russell T. (2013). A Modest Proposal on Method. *Method & Theory in the Study of Religion*, 25(4–5), 339–49.

McGinn, Bernard (2008). Regina Quondam . . .. *Speculum*, 83(4), 817–39.

McGrath, Alister (2007). *The Dawkins Delusion? Atheist Fundamentalism and Denial of the Divine.* London: SPCK.

Mendenhall, Allen (2013). From Natural Law to Natural Inferiority: The Construction of Racist Jurisprudence in Early Virginia. *PEER English* (8), https://ssrn.com/abstract=2214462.

Messer, Neil (2020). *Science in Theology: Encounters between and the Christian Tradition*. London: T&T Clark.

Milbank, John (2000). The Conflict of the Faculties: Theology and the Economy of the Sciences. Mark Theisson Nation and Samuel Wells, eds., *Faithfulness and Fortitude: Conversations with the Theological Ethics of Stanley Hauerwas*. Edinburgh: T&T Clark, 39–58.

Milbank, John (2006). *Theology & Social Theory: Beyond Secular Reason*. Malden, MA: Blackwell.

Mulieris Dignitatem (1988). Vatican. www.vatican.va/content/john-paul-ii/en/apost_letters/1988/documents/hf_jp-ii_apl_19880815_mulieris-dignitatem.html.

Murphy, Nancey (1985). A Niebuhruan Typology for the Relation of Theology to Science. *Pacific Theological Review*, 18(3), 16–23.

Murphy, Nancey (1996). *Beyond Liberalism and Fundamentalism: How Modern and Postmodern Philosophy Set the Theological Agenda*. Harrisburg, PA: Trinity Press International.

Neurath, Otto (1931/1983). Sociology in the Framework of Physicalism. R.S. Cohen and M. Meurath, eds., *Philosophical Papers* 1913–1946. Vienna Circle Collection, vol.16. Dordrecht: Springer.

Newman, John Henry (1979). *The Idea of a University: Defined and Illustrated*. Oxford: Clarendon Press.

Newton, William (2020). Why Aquinas's Metaphysics of Gender is Fundamentally Correct: A Response to John Finley. *Linacre*, 87(2), 198–205.

Nielsen, Kai (1967). Wittgensteinian Fideism. *Philosophy*, 42(161), 191–209.

Numbers, Ronald, ed. (2009). *Galileo Goes to Jail: And Other Myths About Science and Religion*. Cambridge, MA: Harvard University Press.

Numbers, Ronald (2010). Simplifying Complexity: Patterns in the History of Science and Religion. Thomas Dixon, Geoffrey Cantor and Stephen Pumfrey, eds., *Science and Religion: New Historical Perspectives*. Cambridge: Cambridge University Press, 263–82.

Nuttall, Geoffrey (1992). *Holy Spirit in Puritan Faith and Experience*. Chicago, IL: University of Chicago Press.

O'Conner, Flannery (1986). *The Correspondence of Flannery O'Connor and the Brainerd Cheneys*. C. Ralph Stephens, ed. Jackson, MS: University Press of Mississippi.

Owen, John (2017). *Divine Original of the Scriptures of the Integrity and Purity of the Hebrew and Greek Text*. London: FB&C.

Peacocke, Arthur R. (1933). *Theology for a Scientific Age: Being and Becoming – Natural, Divine and Human*. Minneapolis, MN: Fortress Press.

Peacocke, Arthur R. (1981). *The Sciences and Theology in the Twentieth Century.* Notre Dame, IN: Notre Dame University Press.

Peacocke, Arthur R. (1993). *Theology for a Scientific Age: Being and Becoming-Natural, Divine and Human.* Minnaepolis: Fortress Press.

Pedersen, Daniel J. (2021). Is It Just for God to Damn for Sins Which Have Evolutionary Causes? *Theological Puzzles* (1). www.theo-puzzles.ac.uk/2021/03/26/dpedersen/.

Perry, John (2021). Can Intersex Persons be Ordained as Catholic Priests? *Theological Puzzles* (2). www.theo-puzzles.ac.uk/2021/06/05/jperry/.

Perry, John and Leidenhag, Joanna (2021). What is Science-Engaged Theology. *Modern Theology*, 37(2): 245–53.

Perry, John and Ritchie, Sarah Lane (2018). Magnets, Magic, and Other Anomalies: In Defense of Methodological Naturalism. *Zygon: Journal of Religion and Science*, 53(4), 1064–93.

Peters, Ted, ed. (1998). *Science & Theology: The New Consonance.* Boulder, CO: Westview Press.

Popper, Karl (1963). *Conjectures and Refutations: The Growth of Scientific Knowledge.* London: Routledge.

Popper, Karl (2002). *The Logic of Scientific Discovery.* Abingdon: Routledge.

Putnam, Hilary and Oppenheimer, Paul (1958). Unity of Science as a Working Hypothesis. *Minnesota Studies in the Philosophy of Science*, 2, 2–36.

Rehman, Rashad (2022). What is Intersex? A Reply to Perry's Applied Moral Theology of Sex, Intersex and Ordination, *Theological Puzzles* (7). www.theo-puzzles.ac.uk/2022/05/02/rehman/.

Rasmusson, Arne (2021). Radical Orthodoxy on Catholicism, Protestantism and Liberalism/Liberality: On the Use of Historical Narratives and Quantitative Methods in Political Theology. *Modern Theology*, 37(1), 44–61.

Ratzinger, Joseph (2003). *Circular Letter to All Presidents of the Episcopal Conferences Concerning the Use of Low-Gluten Altar Breads and Mustum as Matter for the Celebration of the Eucharist.* Vatican: Congregation for the Doctrine of Faith. www.vatican.va/roman_curia/congregations/cfaith/documents/rc_con_cfaith_doc_20030724_pane-senza-glutine_en.html.

Richardson, Alan (2006). The Many Unities of Science. Longion Kellert, Helen Longino and C. Kenneth Waters, eds., *Scientific Pluralism*. Minneapolis, MN: University of Minnesota Press, 1–25.

Rorty, Richard (1988). Is Natural Science a Natural Kind?. Ernan McMullan, ed., *Construction and Constraint: The Shaping of Scientific Rationality.* South Bend, IN: University of Notre Dame Press, 49–65.

Runia, David T. (1986). *Philo of Alexandria and the Timaeus of Plato.* Leiden: E.J. Brill.

Russell, Robert John (1985). A Critical Appraisal of Peacocke's Thought on Religion and Science. *Religion Intellectual Life*, 2(4), 48–51.

Scrutton, Tasia (2021). Can a Period of Mental Distress be Both a Dark Night of the Soul and a Mental Illness at the Same Time? *Theological Puzzles* (2). www.theo-puzzles.ac.uk/2021/06/05/tscrutton/.

Shively, Elizabeth and Rüggemeier, Jan (2021). Cognitive Linguistics and New Testament Narrative: Investigating Methodology through Characterization. *Biblical Interpretation: A Journal of Contemporary Approaches*, 29(4–5), 403–634.

Sollereder, Bethany (2021). Can Theology Help Us Understand the Human Role in Environmental Restoration? *Theological Puzzles* (3). www.theo-puzzles.ac.uk/2021/08/28/bsollereder/.

Soskice, Janet (2022). Science, Beauty, and the Creative Word. Peter Harrison and John Milbank, eds., *After Science and Religion: Fresh Perspectives from Philosophy and Theology*. Cambridge: Cambridge University Press, 144–54.

Stenhouse, John. (2019). Christian Missionaries, Science, and the Complexity Thesis in the Nineteenth-Century World. Bernard Lightman, ed., *Rethinking History, Science, And Religion*. Pittsburgh, Pennsylvania: University of Pittsburgh Press, 65–84.

Stout, Jeffery (2004). *Democracy and Tradition*. Princeton, NJ: Princeton University Press.

Strawn, Brent A. (2017). *The Old Testament is Dying: A Diagnosis and Recommended Treatment*. Grand Rapids, MI: Baker Academic.

Suppes, Patrick (1993). *Models and Methods in the Philosophy of Science: Selected Essays*. Dordrecht: Springer.

Tanner, Kathryn (1994). The Difference Theological Anthropology Makes. *Theology Today*, 50(4), 567–79.

Tanner, Kathryn (1997). *Theories of Culture: A New Agenda for Culture*. Minneapolis, MN: Fortress Press.

Tanner, Kathryn (2010). *Christ the Key*. Cambridge: Cambridge University Press.

Tanner, Kathryn (2019). Shifts in Theology Over the Last Quarter Century. *Modern Theology*, 26(1), 39–44.

Tausen, Brittany, and Douglass, Katherine. (2021). Can the Tools of Social-Cognitive Psychology Inform Spiritual Formation Practices? *Theological Puzzles* (4). www.theo-puzzles.ac.uk/2021/10/21/tausen-douglass/.

Tonstad, Linn Marie (2020). (Un)wise Theologians: Systematic Theology in the University. *International Journal of Systematic Theology*, 22(4), 494–511.

Vanhoozer, Kevin J. (2005). *The Drama of Doctrine: A Canonical-Linguistic Approach to Christian Theology*. Louisville, KY: Westminster John Knox Press.

Webster, John (2011). Regina Artium: Theology and the Humanities. Christopher Craig Brittain and Francesca Aran Murphy, eds., *Theology, University, Humanities: Initium Sapientiae Timor Domini*. Eugene, OR: Cascade, 39–63.

Webster, John (2016). *Confessing God: Essays in Christian Dogmatics*, 2nd vol. London: T&T Clark.

Wesley, John (2016). *The Book of Discipline of the United Methodist Church*. London: United Methodist Publishing House.

Whewell, William (1834). Mrs Sommerville on the Connexion of the Physical Sciences. *Quarterly Review*, 51(2–3), 54–67. https://babel.hathitrust.org/cgi/ssd?id=mdp.39015074711394;seq=64;num=54.

Whitehead, Alfred North (1925). Religion and Science. *The Atlantic* (August).

Wood, William (2017). *Analytic Theology and the Academic Study of Religion*. Oxford: Oxford University Press.

Wright, Nicholas Thomas (2019). *History and Eschatology: Jesus and the Promise of Natural Theology*. London: SPCK.

Zahl, Simeon (2020). *The Holy Spirit and Christian Experience*. Oxford: Oxford University Press.

Zahl, Simeon (2021). Beyond the Critique of Soteriological Individualism: Relationality and Social Cognition. *Modern Theology*, 37(2): 336–61.

Zahl, Simeon (2022). Theological Anthropology and Psychological Science: Prospects and Challenges. *Society for the Study of Theology*, 29 March. Warwick: University of Warwick.

Zakai, Avihu (2007). The Rise of Modern Science and the Decline of Theology as the 'Queen of the Sciences' in the Early Modern Era. *Reformation & Renaissance Review*, 9(2), 125–51.

Ziman, John and Midgley, Mary (2001). Pluralism in Science. *Interdisciplinary Science Reviews*, 26(3), 153.

Acknowledgements

In May 2022, the manuscript that would become this Element was the subject of a day-long seminar in Ålesund, Norway. We owe thanks to all those who took part: Adam Willows, Andrew Davison, Arne Rasmusson, Bethany Sollereder, D. T. Everhart, John Berkman, Justin Barrett, Mark Harris, Meghan Page, and Sarah Lane Ritchie. Parts of Sections 2 and 5 were presented at a research seminar for The Faraday Institute for Science and Religion in October 2021, and an earlier version of Section 4 was presented at the History and Philosophy of Science research seminar at the University of Leeds in March 2022. We thank all those who asked probing questions and made helpful suggestions at these events. Our involvement in this field has greatly benefitted from a related grant, 'New Visions in Theological Anthropology' hosted at the University of St Andrews and supported by the John Templeton Foundation. This Element would never have existed without the assistance of Sterling Yates (Project Manager), Dorothy Campbell (Administrator), Kevin Nordby (Teaching Advisor), and more than sixty Fellows in Science-Engaged Theology who taught us so much over three years. Mikael Leidenhag (Science & Theology Editor) commissioned the many examples that bring our text to light by showing how science-engaged theology really works. D. T. Everhart (Research Associate) masterfully handled the citations.

For our parents.

Cambridge Elements $^{\equiv}$

Christianity and Science

Andrew Davison
University of Cambridge

Andrew Davison is the Starbridge Associate Professor in Theology and Science at the University of Cambridge. He is Fellow of Corpus Christi College and Dean of the Chapel, and looks after the arts and humanities work of the Leverhulme Centre for Life in the Universe at the University of Cambridge.

Editorial Board

About the Series

The Elements series on Christianity and Science will offer an authoritative presentation of scholarship in this interdisciplinary field of inquiry. Opening new avenues for study and research, the series will highlight several issues, notably the importance of historical scholarship for understanding the relationship between Christianity and natural science, and the vital role played by philosophy in this field today.

Cambridge Elements ☰

Christianity and Science

Elements in the Series

Printed in the United States
by Baker & Taylor Publisher Services